LEVELING

THE

PLAYING

FIELD

LEVELING
THE
PLAYING
FIELD

A Guide to Successful Business Development Transactions
for Private and Small Public Life Science Companies

Lawrence P. Horowitz
Larry Ellberger
Jane V. Scott, Ph.D.
Principals of HVA, Inc.

iUniverse, Inc.
New York   Bloomington

Leveling the Playing Field
A Guide to Successful Business Development Transactions for
Private and Small Public Life Science Companies

iUniverse books may be ordered through booksellers or by contacting:

iUniverse
1663 Liberty Drive
Bloomington, IN 47403
www.iuniverse.com
1-800-Authors (1-800-288-4677)

Because of the dynamic nature of the Internet, any Web addresses
or links contained in this book may have changed
since publication and may no longer be valid.

The views expressed in this work are solely those of the author and do not
necessarily reflect the views of the publisher, and the publisher hereby disclaims
any responsibility for them.

ISBN: 978-0-595-51700-8 (pbk)
ISBN: 978-0-595-61998-6 (ebk)

Printed in the United States of America

iUniverse rev. date: 11/24/08

CONTENTS

INTRODUCTION

Small cap life science companies are in the business of discovering innovative technologies, developing these technologies into successful products, and realizing value from their technology innovations. Small cap life science companies include start-up, early-stage and pre-IPO private companies, and public companies with small market capitalizations. Most focus on R&D, rather than manufacturing and market. Small cap life science companies will be referred to as Small Companies.

Business development transactions—out-licensing, strategic partnerships, acquisitions—are how many Small Companies realize value from their innovations. Business development transactions can realize value from technology in several ways. These transactions allow access to large, global life science companies' development, clinical, regulatory, manufacturing and commercial resources; generate cash-flow often with minimal dilution to the Small Company's investors, and provide independent validation of the technology. Large global companies have significant sales and a full range of development, regulatory, clinical, manufacturing, and marketing resources. Large global companies will be referred to as Large Companies.

How much value is realized from a transaction depends on the technology and on the Small Company's business development process. We leave technology development to scientists, engineers, and clinicians. We know about business development transactions and the business development process. We wrote *Leveling the Playing Field* to share our expertise and experience to help Small Companies improve their business development process and thereby realize more value from their technology.

A business development transaction, as used throughout this Guide, is an agreement whereby a Large Company acquires the Small Company or acquires rights to a Small Company's technology with the intent of developing the technology into a commercial product. The Small Company thereby sells (sells or licenses) its technology to a buyer (buyer or licensee), a Large Company. The financial terms of the transaction—e.g., upfront payment, milestone payments, and royalties—constitute the price the Large Company pays to buy the technology and the value the Small Company realizes from selling the technology. The buying and selling of technology which occurs in a business development transaction is similar to many buyer/seller transactions. Understanding buyer/seller transactions can help business development transaction dynamics.

The price the buyer pays to acquire an item for sale (or, looked at from the other side of the table, the price the seller realizes from selling the item) represents a compromise between the seller's desire to maximize value received and the buyer's desire to minimize value paid. Whether the compromise favors the buyer or the seller depends on how circumstances tilt the playing field to the advantage of one side or the other. Small Companies are sellers in business development transactions; we will focus on what benefits them. The playing field is tilted to the advantage of sellers when: (1) there are few, if any, other sellers with equivalent products, (2) the items for sale are in short supply, (3) potential buyers put a high value on acquiring the items, (4) there are many potential buyers, and (5) the seller is under no pressure to sell now. Seller cartels, OPEC being a successful example, tilt the playing field in their favor by exploiting each of the above five factors. With a sharply tilted playing field, OPEC delivers high revenues for its members and inflicts high prices on oil consumers.

What about negotiations? Don't skilled negotiators always get the best price regardless of which direction and by how much the playing field is tilted? Negotiations always take place within the context of the tilted playing field. When the tilt is steep, negotiating skills can have limited effect. OPEC has tilted the field to its advantage. Powerful and skilled negotiators from oil buyers have not been able to prevent OPEC's ability to raise prices.

Negotiating skills, in and of themselves, can only make the best of how the playing field is laid out. The potential yield from negotiating skills is limited by degree of tilt. The steeper the tilt the less negotiating skills can accomplish. In a perfectly level playing field, negotiating skills have an enormous effect on outcomes. Analogously, football fields are made level so that the athletes determine the final score. A tilted field would off-set the skills and abilities of the athletes.

Negotiating skills do matter. A skilled negotiator for the stronger party imposes his demands on the weaker party. A skilled negotiator for the weaker side limits how far the stronger side can impose itself. The tilt of the playing field limits what a negotiator can accomplish, no matter how good her skills.

The playing field for the "game" between the Small Company and the Large Company tilts to the advantage of the Large Company. At the outset, every advantage weighs in on the side of the Large Company. Small Companies do not have to accept this unfavorable tilt passively. The ability of the Small Company to level the playing field is the central premise of this Guide. While it is not always possible for the Small Company to tilt the field to its advantage, it is always possible to have a more level playing field, thereby improving the Small Company's ability to negotiate favorable transaction terms.

The Small Company levels the playing field by creating circumstances which favor the seller. Circumstances which we identified above as favoring the seller are: (1) there are few, if any, other sellers with equivalent products, (2) the items for sale are in short supply, (3) potential buyers put a high value on acquiring the items for sale, (4) there are many potential buyers, and (5) the seller is under no pressure to sell. Convincing Large Companies that the technology is unique, has intellectual property protection, and has the potential to become a large, successful commercial product accomplishes (1), (2), and (3). Engaging several Large Companies interested in acquiring the technology, and communicating that the Small Company does not need to do a transaction accomplishes (4) and (5). Creating a level playing field has to be done prior to the start of negotiations.

Leveling the Playing Field describes an approach to business development which, when properly executed, can create substantial negotiating strength for the seller. HVA's approach to business development is based on two principles. First for the Small Company, an auction is the most effective way to structure a business development effort. Life science business development is never, as far as we know, done as a formal auction. We are certainly not recommending a formal auction mechanism. Our approach has enough similarities to a formal auction that we will use the term auction throughout. Second, information about its technology is the Small Company's most valuable asset to creating a level playing field.

Competition among potential buyers to acquire a scarce, valuable asset works to the advantage of the seller. Creating competition can be best accomplished by the Small Company holding an auction. Auctions have been studied extensively by economists. Government auctions of broad band spectrums were the driving force behind auction theory. The resulting auction theory describes how an auction can best be conducted under a wide range of conditions. The theory's conclusions can be applied more broadly, including, as we shall see, to business development. This Guide uses auction theory's important conclusions to support and reinforce its major points. We have drawn heavily on two primary sources of information about auction theory: *Auction Theory* by Vijay Krishna and *Putting Auctions to Work* by Paul Milgrom. Details are in the bibliography.

The potential for an auction to level the playing field depends to a great extent on potential buyers' access to information about the object for sale. Information first attracts potential buyers and then builds their interest in and enthusiasm for acquiring the object. Information allows potential buyers to value the object for sale appropriately. Knowing that their competitors have the same information and are therefore likely to attach a similar value to the object induces potential buyers to bid aggressively rather than risk losing out. Not surprisingly, an auction's potential depends directly on the quality and quantity of information available to potential buyers.

In the life science business, information about the technology—the underlying science, results of experiments, animal studies, clinical studies, and intellectual property—motivates Large Companies to want to acquire the technology at a high price. Information, as used throughout this Guide, means information supported by data. (This very important definition of information appears repeatedly as a reminder.) How effectively the Small Company develops and makes use of this information determines as much as or more than any other factor its ability to level the playing field.

Using information effectively requires an understanding of how Large Companies make technology acquisition decisions. Section I of *Leveling the Playing Field* describes the decision making process of Large Companies. The focus is on the role information plays at each stage of the Large Companies' multi-layered decision making process. Section I also discusses why the playing field starts out tilted so much to the advantage of the Large Company.

Auctions and what makes them powerful are discussed in Section II. Section III shows how applying what makes auctions powerful to life science business development transactions can create significant advantages for the Small Company. Section IV addresses four specific issues: when to hold an "auction", what to do if the "auction fails", how to manage the business development process, and choosing the right global partner. Key points throughout this Guide are illustrated by case studies; all are from our experience. Specifics, including company names, products, and names of individuals have been left out or modified as required to honor confidentiality obligations.

Leveling the Playing Field is the result of the combined business development experience of HVA's principals in the pharmaceutical, biotech, and medical device industries. We have closed 85 life science transactions ranging in size from $2 million to multi-billion. Our transaction track record includes out-licensing, sale of technology, joint development, distribution, and acquisition transactions with companies located in the U.S., Europe, and Asia.

We have all been senior business development executives at Large Companies and know from first-hand experience how Large Companies make technology acquisition decisions; who is involved in these decisions; and what determines whether the answer is "Yes" or "No." Our Large Company business development experience is complemented by our working on transactions as senior executives in R&D, finance, and operations. Having worked at and consulted with Small Companies and the tech transfer offices of major teaching hospitals, we know the importance of closing a transaction and the difficulty of working with Large Companies. In all, our combined life science industry experience makes us uniquely qualified to write *Leveling the Playing Field*.

Leveling the Playing Field is a Guide, not an instruction manual. Our intent is to provide Small Companies with principles and ideas that may be tailored to each transaction.

THE LARGE COMPANY

CHAPTER 1

A TILTED PLAYING FIELD

Large Companies, knowing they have the advantage from the outset, do as much as they can to use their advantage in their business development activities. Small Companies may fail to realize what they are up against. Believing that their technology and their negotiating skills can level the playing field enough for them to get an acceptable transaction, they are frequently disappointed.

As a starting point, every Small Company should recognize that Large Companies have a large number of financial, legal, scientific, clinical, regulatory, marketing and business development executives available to work on a transaction. The number of these functional specialists in the largest of the Large Companies exceeds the total number of people in most Small Companies. Large Companies close many transactions each year and consider as many as twenty opportunities for every one they close. Their business development teams are deep and experienced.

Large Companies have a wide selection of growth opportunities, some from their internal R&D and others from potential transactions with Small Companies. A Small Company's technology is just one of the Large Company's many alternatives. With a wide array of choices, Large Companies often believe they can walk away from any transaction, pursue other growth opportunities, and suffer no adverse consequences. These are opportunities with long-term results. No one gets fired if he passes on an opportunity today that is successful five to fifteen years in the future. Being able to walk away without regret confers an enormous advantage on the Large Company.

With many growth opportunities competing for each Large Company's available resources, combined with decision makers' need for input from many functional groups (R&D, clinical, marketing, finance, etc.), Large Companies move slowly and deliberately. Setting up meetings can take months. Completing what would appear to be routine Confidential Non-Disclosure Agreements and Material Transfer Agreements can take so long that one wonders how long it will take to reach a definitive agreement when the parties get down to serious negotiations. Large Companies sometimes appear to lose interest entirely only to reappear as interested parties a few months later. Small Companies that push for a faster response are reminded of the large number of opportunities the Large Company is considering.

Small Companies are in the opposite position. They have few business development resources—usually an overworked CEO and sometimes an almost equally overworked VP of Business Development. Even when these people are highly skilled, they can be overpowered by the sheer number of equally highly skilled professionals on the Large Company's side of the table.

Whereas a Large Company rarely feels compelled to do any one transaction, the Small Company may be focused on closing one transaction. And, closing that one transaction usually has important ramifications for the Small Company. The Small Company may be able to walk away from any one Large Company. It is unlikely to be able to walk away from all of them.

Small Companies are at the mercy of the pace at set by the Large Companies. Little can be done to accelerate the pace in the large majority of cases. While the Large Company moves ahead deliberately, the pressure on the Small Company to do a transaction increases. By the time a proposal comes from the Large Company, the Small Company may be under so much pressure that it has difficulty walking away or risking further delays by pushing for better terms than those offered.

A Tilted Playing Field

	Large Company	Small Company
Business development resources	Extensive, experienced, dedicated	Few, multi-tasking
Speed/sense of urgency	Slow, often glacial	Now, if not sooner
Alternatives	Many, both in-house and external	Few
Importance	Generally not essential	High to essential

In any book on negotiations, you will find that the party with no need to close a transaction quickly, with acceptable alternatives, and with the ability to walk away has significantly more negotiating strength than the party with pressure to close, with few if any acceptable alternatives, and with no or very limited ability to walk away. Each of the factors that create negotiating strength sits on the Large Company's side of the chart. Combining these factors with the inherent strengths of the Large Company's experienced business development team results in a playing field which can seem nearly vertical to many Small Companies.

Large Companies use the tilted playing field to negotiate transaction terms that give them the best potential return on their spending to acquire, develop, and commercialize the technology. This is exactly what they should be doing. Their investment to acquire the technology combined with the time, expense and risks to have a successful commercial product puts considerable pressure on the Large Company to do transactions markedly in their favor.

A Large Company's objectives for a business development transaction can be, and most often are, quite different from those of a Small Company. Having a tilted playing field gives the Large Company the leverage to have the final transaction terms favor its objectives. Differences in objectives between Large and Small Companies are shown on the table at the end of this chapter.

Symptoms of transactions favoring Large Companies include: no or minimal up-front payments, milestone payments which do not nearly reflect the step-up in value created by achieving the milestones, a weak commitment from the Large Company to commercialize the acquired technology, continuing rights to acquire or develop competing technologies, no significant penalties should the Large Company not live up to its commitments to develop the technology. In such a one-sided transaction, the Large Company gets a disproportionate share of the benefits and the Small Company gets a disproportionate share of the risks.

Transaction Objectives: Large Company–Small Company

Objective	Large Company	Small Company
Total Value of the Transaction	Small	Large
Transaction Structure	Most of payments at back-end: late milestone payments and royalties	Payments at front-end: upfront payments and early milestone payments
Commitment to Develop the Technology	Can be very low	Very high
Termination Rights	No limitations on the right to terminate; no or minimal residual payments	Very limited rights to terminate; large residual payment
Field of Use	As many as possible	As few as possible
Rights to I. P.	As broad as possible	As narrow as necessary
Rights to Future I. P.	Yes	No
Ability to Acquire or Develop Competing Technologies	Yes	No

CHAPTER 2

LARGE COMPANIES' TECHNOLOGY ACQUISITION DECISIONS

The Small Company cannot amass the resources to offset the tilt of the playing field which is so much to the advantage of the Large Company. What the Small Company has is information (information supported by data) about its technology. The Small Company must create advantages for itself by using this information to attract Large Companies' interests and then stimulate their enthusiasm for acquiring the technology. Understanding how Large Companies make decisions about technology is critical to knowing how to make best use of information.

The View from the Large Company's Side of the Table

"… the challenge of auction design can only be understood by
studying the demands of the participants."
Paul Milgrom, *Putting Auction Theory to Work*

Large Companies are interested in acquiring technologies. Everyone in the life science industry is well aware that Small Companies make a disproportionate share of innovations. Large Companies need access to these innovations to maintain their growth, and thereby enhance their stock price.

Interest in acquiring innovative technology is balanced by financial concerns. And addressing financial concerns explains, in part, the deliberate pace of Large Companies. Acquisition of a technology can commit a Large

13

Company to spending tens or hundreds of millions of dollars on development and commercialization. Upfront and milestone payments add to the cost of developing the technology into a commercially successful product. Royalties subtract from the benefits of success.

More often than not, a technology acquisition turns out to be a bad decision. Either the technology fails somewhere in development, in which case the return is negative, or the resulting product lacks the characteristics to be a block buster, in which case the return falls well below expectations. For the Large Company, a technology acquisition is a huge commitment with significant uncertainty about the outcome. All life science R&D projects require a commitment of resources with a high uncertainty in outcome. Acquisition of a technology is more so. The upfront payment and milestone payments add to the expense of development and royalties subtract from the rewards of success. In addition, acquisition of a technology may impose constraints on the Large Company, e.g., limited ability to acquire or develop competing technologies, which can be seen as an additional cost.

Failure, even for products in late-stage clinical trials, occurs frequently. Following are FierceBiotech headlines about drugs failing human clinical trials for a three week period of March 2007.

Liponex shares hammered on trial failure 3/9/07
Advair (Glaxo) fails to hit goal in COPD trial 3/16/07
AtheroGenics' shares plunge after trial failure 3/19/07
Corcept drug misses endpoint in Phase III trials 3/20/07
Intermune slashes staff on heals of trial failure 3/20/07
Amgen shutter Vectibex trial on safety questions 3/23/07
J&J, Otsuka drugs fail heart trials 3/26/07
BioCryst shares slide on trial suspension news 3/27/07
CombinatoRx reports failure of Phase II RA trial 3/27/07
FDA regulators question effectiveness of Provenge (Dendron) 3/27/07.

Failures of research programs and technologies in pre-clinical development which are rarely announced occur with even greater frequency.

The technology acquisition decision is further complicated by the fact Large Companies cannot afford to take on every interesting growth opportunity. Choosing to develop a technology is a major long-term commitment. And, the decision to acquire a technology may preclude or make it very expensive to acquire a better technology in parallel or later on. Choosing not to develop a technology means losing the ability to take advantage of that technology's potential. The need to make choices in the face of very high levels of uncertainty adds to the degree of caution and deliberation exercised by Large Companies.

Deciding whether it wants or needs a technology, and if so, how to value the technology, the Large Company compares the technology to its available alternatives. Though often implicit, the key questions for the Large Company are: "How much will this technology increase the likelihood of developing a commercially successful product compared to my alternatives?" and "What are the major risks?"

Risk is the likelihood of a technology failing to yield a commercially successful product. Development, clinical trial, and regulatory factors are those affecting whether the technology yields a product that gets regulatory approval to commercialize. Intellectual property factors capture whether the technology and resulting product will infringe someone else's intellectual property and the strength of the intellectual property in limiting competitors' abilities to come to market with a similar product. Commercial factors reflect how well the product will perform when and if it comes to market. In addition to the usual market and competitive considerations, commercial factors increasingly include those related to reimbursement. Costs are the development, clinical, and regulatory spending required to bring a new product to market, and the required investment in manufacturing and commercial expenses.

The Role of the Large Company's Scientists, Engineers, and Clinicians

Scientific, technical, and clinical information are needed to answer: "How much will this technology increase the likelihood of developing a commercially successful product compared to my alternatives?" and "What are the major risks?" Two important corollaries flow from this observation. First, unlike market, competitor, and reimbursement information, the Small Company is almost always the primary source of scientific, technical, and clinical information about its technology. Second, the Large Company's scientists, engineers, and clinicians have the responsibility of assessing this information. To create well-informed potential buyers, the Small Company, first and foremost, needs to focus on the information needs of this group.

The needs of this group are scientific, technical, and clinical information supported by data. Understanding this point is critical to understanding this Guide. The Large Company's scientists, engineers, and clinicians have been educated and trained to make decisions based on data. The larger the quantity and the better the quality of the supporting data, the more positive response it elicits from this critical audience. Conversely, limited data or data of poor quality likely elicits either an unfavorable response or a request for additional information.

Information provided to the Large Companies' scientists, engineers, and clinicians should address the following frequently asked questions.

Preclinical/Development

What evidence/data are there that the technology has a reasonable likelihood of yielding a commercially successful product?
How far along is the technology?
What critical development, experiments and animal trials are needed to move into human clinical studies?
Which of the above is most likely to cause the project to fail?

Clinical

What clinical trials have been completed and what do the results of these trials show?
What clinical trials will be needed to achieve regulatory approval in major markets?
How much time and money will be needed to complete these clinical trials?
How likely is it that these clinical trials will achieve end points that in addition to achieving regulatory approval will also support reimbursement claims and create a competitive

advantage? (Or, how likely is it that we will sell enough of the product once regulatory approval is achieved?)

What challenges will human clinical trials face in terms of signing up investigators and enlisting patients?

The Role of the Large Company's Business Development Professionals

Business development has responsibility for carrying out the process of acquiring new products and technologies. Coordinating the assessment of the technology and communicating with the Small Company are primary business development functions. As part of this, business development is the gate keeper for every external opportunity. Business development's gate keeping function includes opportunities identified by the Large Company's scientists, engineers, and clinicians. Opportunities are almost always championed by scientists, engineers, and clinicians; business development rarely champions an acquisition of a product or technology.

The decision whether or not to acquire a technology is in the hands of the Large Company's scientists, engineers, clinicians, and senior management. Business development often participates in the decision, but not as the final decision maker. On the other hand, business development can reject opportunities outside of their company's strategic areas of interest.

Other functions of business development vary from company to company and sometimes among operating units of the same company. Functions that may be taken on by business development include: financial valuation of the opportunity, negotiating terms of the agreement, prospecting for new opportunities, and participating in the determination of their company's area of strategic interest.

The Role of the Large Company's CEO

Some Small Companies believe that Large Company's CEOs make immediate decisions regarding the technology. More than one Small Company CEO has demanded that we get him in front of the CEO of Merck, Pfizer, Johnson & Johnson, GSK, Boston Scientific, or any one of the other Large Companies to pitch his technology. "Once the CEO sees what we have, the deal will be as good as done" is a phrase we hear from some of our Small Company clients. If it were only that easy! (Not that getting an appointment with a Large Company CEO is easy.)

Senior executives of Large Companies make decisions about a technology only when the technology has been thoroughly evaluated and enthusiastically supported by their company's scientific, technical, clinical, regulatory, and marketing people.

Three Stages of Decision Making—Three Levels of Information

To decide whether or not to acquire a technology and how much to pay for it, a Large Company goes through three stages of decision making: (1) is the technology of any potential interest to us at all?, (2) what is the potential value of the technology to us?, and (3) before we sign the contract are we sure the Small Company has given us all of the facts and nothing but the facts? Each of these three stages requires a different level of information. These three stages match with the information that should be provided, in (1) the Non-Confidential Executive Summary, (2) Confidential Presentations and Dossiers, and (3) in legal, technical and financial due diligence. Our discussion of the objective of each of the three decision making stages and the information required follows. The specific issue of disclosing confidential information is discussed in Chapter 6.

The Non-Confidential Executive Summary provides information to allow the Large Company to decide that the technology is of potential interest to them. Large Companies assess opportunities of potential interest carefully. A serious evaluation of a new technology requires diverting the efforts of senior scientists, engineers, and clinicians from their current projects. Marketing, financial, legal, and business development staff also become engaged in a serious new technology evaluation. Those evaluating a Non-Confidential Executive Summary have a strong negative bias as a consequence. No one wants to be responsible for wasting their co-workers' time. Not-Invented-Here adds to the negative bias. Unfortunately, changing this is beyond the capability of even the best written Non-Confidential Executive Summary.

Before initiating a full-scale evaluation, the Large Company builds a consensus that there is a real possibility that the technology being considered has substantial value to them. One or two "Nos" usually means that there is little hope for a consensus. Once this happens, the ability of the Small Company to turn this around is limited. It does happen, but only very infrequently. The objective of the Non-Confidential Executive Summary is to minimize the likelihood of one or two people in the organization saying "No." Appendix A has three non-confidential Executive Summaries that have been successful in generating serious interest from Large Companies.

Information in Confidential Presentations and Confidential Dossiers must pass the stiffer requirement of getting people to say "Yes!" A "Yes!" means the Large Company has decided it wants to acquire the Small Company's technology subject to the outcome of legal and financial due diligence and being able to obtain satisfactory terms. As discussed previously, a "Yes" means that the Large Company has committed to devoting its R&D, clinical, and marketing resources to development and commercialization of the technology.

Getting to a final "Yes" often means approval from the Large Company's senior management, and for larger transactions, the Large Company's Board of Directors. By and large, senior management and Boards of Directors rely on their senior scientists and engineers to verify that the technology has value. Financial and business development staff responsible for working out the acquisition price and transaction terms also rely on senior scientists, clinicians, and engineers for estimates of the time and cost required to go from the technology's state at the time of acquisition through to regulatory approval. The financial and business development staff looks to these same individuals to assess the risk of failure.

Legal and financial due diligence, the final step, is an in-depth audit of the Small Company's records, contracts, and regulatory filings. Information, clearly, plays a central role here. As legal and financial due diligence typically occurs immediately before closing a transaction, it is outside the scope of this Guide.

Financial Projections

HVA advises against putting financial projections into most Non-Confidential Executive Summaries or confidential information packages. We know from personal experience that Small Company financial projections are usually ignored by the Large Company. Large Companies have their own experts who may not have the, sometimes unwarranted, enthusiasm of those preparing the Small Companies' projections. Estimates of what it takes to bring a product to market come from R&D and clinical affairs. Estimates of sales and selling prices come from Marketing.

Executives at some Small Companies believe that their projections become a basis for negotiations. This is a variant of asking for an exorbitant selling price so that the final price can be negotiated down to a level that is still satisfactory to the seller. We all have been on the receiving end of these tactics. They do not work, ever. Large Companies' projections and valuations are done independently of the Small Company's projections and valuations. CFOs, CEOs and Boards of Directors want to know their decisions are based on an objective, realistic valuation of what is being acquired performed by their staff.

We advise against providing financial projections to avoid the, admittedly remote, possibility of our Small Company client under-estimating the value of its technology. Should this happen, the Small Company is very likely to leave serious money on the table. Finally, we have, while at Large Companies, been in too many presentations where the Small Company's financial projections caused unnecessary debates. We have found that our clients are much better off giving compelling reasons why their technology should be valued as a singular asset and let the Large Company value the technology themselves.

There is one exception to our advising clients to exclude financial projections—a technology that could create a new market, could revitalize a stagnant market, or could change significantly how patients are treated. Here, the technology has the very real potential to deviate from industry norms. The Small Company should demonstrate the financial returns from this potential. The Small Company has to make a very strong case for how its technology would deviate from industry norms for its projections to be taken seriously.

AUCTIONS AND BUSINESS DEVELOPMENT TRANSACTIONS

CHAPTER 3

WHY AN AUCTION?

An auction, by revealing potential buyers' eagerness to buy and by creating competition among potential buyers, creates power for the seller far in excess of what the seller is ever likely to get in one-on-one interactions with individual potential buyers. Auctions, because of their ability to create power for the seller, are used to get the highest price in everything from agricultural commodities, to repossessed cars, to real estate, to rare works of art. An auction can do the same for Small Companies.

Auctions are especially advantageous to the seller when several potential buyers are competing for a singular asset, e.g., a Rembrandt or an ideally situated piece of real estate. Potential buyers wanting ownership of the singular asset must compete with each other in a winner-take-all contest. The highest bidder gets the asset; the others go home empty handed. Those who go home empty handed are unlikely to see the asset up for auction anytime soon, if ever. The more important the singular asset is to potential buyers' emotional or financial well-being, the greater the competition and the higher the final selling price.

How a singular asset affects buyers' behaviors has been long recognized. Spinoza, the 17th century philosopher, writes, "If we imagine that someone enjoys something that only one person can possess, we shall endeavor to bring it about that he does not possess that thing." (Benedictus Spinoza, Ethics, Part 3, Proposition 32; Oxford University Press, 2000·) Spinoza may have overstated the case. Nevertheless, he clearly recognizes that ownership of a singular asset induces competitive behavior.

To emphasize the effect a singular asset has on buyers' behaviors, let us compare the auction of a singular asset with an auction for repossessed cars. Used car dealers and individuals bidding at this auction know that if they do not get the car currently on auction, similar cars will be on auction later in the day or tomorrow. Nobody with the means to pay is ever likely to go home empty handed. And nobody is going to bid up to the last dollar of value for any car.

A Small Company's technology is a singular asset capable of providing "financial well-being" to a Large Company. (What makes a Small Company's technology a singular asset is discussed in Chapter 5.) An auction, therefore, should have similar benefits for the Small Company's technology as for a Rembrandt.

A news release announcing Ligand's sale of its pain product AVINZA is an independent endorsement for "auctions" in life science business development transactions. Italics are the authors'.

Ligand Announces Sale of AVINZA

SAN DIEGO—(BUSINESS WIRE)—Sept. 7, 2006—Ligand Pharmaceuticals Incorporated (NASDAQ:LGND) (the "Company" or "Ligand") announced today that it has signed a definitive asset purchase agreement to transfer the assets associated with AVINZA (morphine sulfate extended-release capsules) to King Pharmaceuticals, Inc. ("King"). The purchase price is a combination of aggregate up-front cash consideration of $313 million, plus a tiered royalty agreement which survives until the patent expiration in November 2017.

"The AVINZA bidding process was a competitive one, and we are pleased that our efforts have resulted in this exciting business opportunity with King," said Henry F. Blissenbach, Ligand Chairman and Interim CEO."

How Auctions Work

Competitive bidding is the most obvious feature of an auction. Every potential buyer knows that there are others also bidding to acquire the asset being sold. In an open auction, where all potential buyers know the most recent bid, a potential buyer continues to bid until: (1) the price is more than he can afford to spend, (2) the previous bid is at a price greater than his perception of the value of the asset, or

(3) every other potential buyer has dropped out. The winner is the potential buyer who puts the highest value on the asset being sold and has the ability to pay that price. The winning bid, in most cases, will be only slightly greater than the next highest bid because everyone in the auction knows what the others have bid. A potential buyer may submit a much higher bid when that buyer is under pressure to close off the auction as quickly as possible.

In sealed bid auctions, potential buyers submit one bid without necessarily knowing who else is participating and with no knowledge of what others have bid. Should even one potential buyer know what others are bidding, that potential buyer will acquire the asset for $1 more than the highest bid submitted by others. Unlike an open auction, other potential buyers generally do not have the opportunity to respond by upping their bids. The selling price, in this situation, is likely to be much less than in an open auction.

When bidders in a sealed bid auction know there is serious competition, their bids will be close to their perceived value for the asset being sold even if they do not know the identity of their competitors. When they do know, or have a good idea, who else is bidding, the competition is an additional motivation for each potential buyer to bid close to their perceived value. Having a good idea of who else is bidding is certainly true in life science where the number of potential buyers is limited and their identities are well known. Bidders, assuming they are truly interested in the asset, bid close to their perceived value rather than risk submitting a lower bid and risk losing out to a bid only slightly greater.

The following case study demonstrates what happens in an auction situation when a potential buyer tries to get a bargain.

Getting Behind the Eight Ball with a Low Ball Bid—Case Study

A specialty pharma company was interested in acquiring a Small Company's late Stage II product for severe chronic pain. With regulatory approval to commercialize, the Small Company's product would complement the specialty pharma company's product line, improve their ability to compete in the market, and allow for a significant expansion of selling effort. The specialty pharma company believed that due to regulatory issues related to pain management products they would be the only bidder.

Believing they had to be the sole bidder, the specialty pharma company submitted a low ball offer. (The financial analysis HVA performed for the Small Company showed that the offer was well below a very conservative estimate of the product's value to the specialty pharma company.)

The specialty pharma company was so certain that they were the only bidder that they told the Small Company that they would not consider any counter-offer. The specialty pharma company reiterated their refusal to consider a counter-offer when they were told the Small Company was in discussions with another potential bidder. The Small Company had no choice but to exclude the specialty pharma company from the auction. The Small Company entered into a transaction with the other bidder, and the specialty pharma company lost an important strategic opportunity.

The effort the specialty pharma company had devoted to evaluating this opportunity indicated they saw it as strategically important. Yet they failed to follow through as evidenced by their low bid. In any event, the auction mechanism allowed the Small Company to find a buyer willing to pay a price consistent with the strategic value of the asset.

Going after a bargain and failing to acquire the asset becomes particularly problematic when bidding on a singular asset. Remember, the singular asset on sale may not ever be for sale again or the next sale may be far into the future. For most bidders, the importance of acquiring a singular asset outweighs the importance of getting a bargain.

This is not to say that a Large Company interested in acquiring technology will never submit a low-ball offer. They may do so when, as in the above case study, they believe they are the only potential buyer. A low ball bid may be submitted when the Large Company believes that the Small Company will respond with a counter-offer or that the Small Company will allow a second bid. In any event, a Small Company that has an effective business development process can push the Large Company to bid close to their perceived value. Large Companies who have decided to submit a term sheet usually do not want to lose out on an opportunity for a relatively small amount of money so they eventually bid close to their perceived value.

Selling Price and Auction Participants

Who participates in an auction can have a great effect on the selling price. For open bid auctions, the selling price is marginally above that of the next to last bid. This is not necessarily the highest price she might be willing to pay. This buyer may have been willing to bid more if she were competing against others who either put a higher value on the asset or could afford to bid more than those who actually participated in the auction. If the buyer would not have been willing to bid more, the participation of more enthusiastic, wealthy buyers could have also resulted in higher selling price. Either way, the seller is likely to get a better price.

Potential buyers in sealed bid auctions bid close to their perceived value of the asset or as much as they can afford. The more enthusiastic, wealthy potential buyers participate the higher the likely selling price. Enthusiastic, wealthy potential buyers will tend to put a high value on the asset for sale and can afford to pay a higher selling price.

A sealed bid auction can result in a higher selling price than an open auction when there is one potential buyer who, for whatever reason, puts a much higher value on a singular asset than other potential buyers. Here, the potential buyer whose valuation greatly exceeds that of other potential buyers will, in a sealed bid auction, put in a very high bid rather than risk being outbid. In an open auction, the selling price will be marginally higher than that of the next to last bid regardless of how high the final buyer's valuation may be.

For example, in an open auction a potential buyer who values the asset being sold at $10,000 will bid only slightly more than the next to last bidder. If the next to last bidder bids $5,000, the buyer will acquire the asset for $5,001. This potential buyer is willing to bid up to $10,000, but will not pay this much unless forced to do so by a bidder who values the asset at a similarly high price. When, for reasons we will discuss next, this potential buyer has a much greater perceived value than others, an open auction allows this buyer to get a bargain. The same buyer in a sealed bid auction does not know what others bid. If this buyer bids less than $10,000, say $7,500, she runs the risk of losing the asset even though she would be willing to pay $10,000 for it. Thus, she will bid $10,000.

Personal and Emotional Factors

A potential buyer puts an extraordinarily high value on an asset when the valuation is affected by personal, emotional, or, in the case of life science, strategic considerations unique to that buyer. Such strategic considerations may include: establishing a position in a new market or market segment, creating a competitive advantage, maintaining an existing franchise, offsetting a competitive disadvantage, adding size to the business to create economies of scale, and acquiring enabling intellectual property. Clearly, finding such a buyer is a big bonus for the seller. The following case study demonstrates how powerful this can be for a life science business development transaction.

A Magic Carpet Ride—Case Study

At an auction of rare Persian rugs, we observed a woman who kept bidding on one rug even when the price went well above the appraised value. Eventually, she out bid everyone else and bought the rug. When the auction was over, we asked the woman why she was willing to pay what seemed to us to be an exorbitant price.

"I've been looking at Persian rugs for years. The rug I just bought was the only one I've seen that fits perfectly with my living room décor. I don't think the price I paid was exorbitant" was her reply.

The auction process allowed this woman to reveal the strength of her personal preferences. No one knows how much more she might have paid had there been another bidder who also saw the rug as a perfect match for her living room décor. And, no one knows how much she might have paid in a sealed bid auction.

Auction houses want personal and emotional factors to affect the selling price as much as possible. Knowing who these buyers are and having as many of them as possible participate makes it very likely that personal and emotional factors will come strongly into play. Providing information about the item for sale helps establish a common "objective" evaluation on top of which personal and emotional factors are added.

Appraisals cannot account for personal and emotional factors. Auction houses provide all potential buyers the facts supporting the "objective" appraisal of the asset. By having all potential buyers at similar starting points, the selling price will be determined by the buyer whose unique personal and emotional factors result in the highest increment above the "objective" appraisal.

Auction theory, which we will discuss in the next section, supports our observation that providing each buyer with all available information results in auctions yielding the highest selling price. The auction houses also widely advertise in media that potential buyers read so that they can attract the greatest number of potential buyers.

Auctions and Information

The importance of information (supported by data) plays a central part in this Guide. The reasons for this follow from the role information plays in having a successful auction, namely information does the following.:

- Attracts potential buyers to the auction
- Builds enthusiasm for acquiring the asset for sale
- Provides a common base for valuation; personal and emotional factors are added to this base.

CHAPTER 4

AUCTION THEORY

Our observations about auctions are well supported by a branch of quantitative economics called auction theory. The mathematics of auction theory are beyond the scope of this Guide. Here, we summarize some of auction theory's important conclusions that reinforce and expand on our previous discussion. Much of what follows is drawn from *Auction Theory* by Vijay Krishna. This and other materials used in this section are referenced in the bibliography.

Dr. Krishna defines a common aspect of auctions and auction-like institutions: "They elicit information, in the form of bids, from potential buyers regarding their willingness to pay, and the outcome—that is who wins and who pays how much—is determined solely on the basis of the received information." In life science business development transactions, term sheets play the role of bids. And the Large Company offering the best terms, that is, the best price, is almost always the winner. Though not perfect, a life science business development transaction fits the definition closely enough for us to draw valuable conclusions from auction theory.

Dr. Krishna points out that uncertainty facing buyers and the seller about the value of the object for sale is an inherent feature of auctions. The seller does not know how high the highest bidder will go or if there will be any bidders at all. The buyers do not know how others in the auction will behave. *Leveling the Playing Field* can be thought of in terms of how to use the uncertainty inherent in auctions to the best advantage of the seller. How sellers use information about the object for sale plays a central role in building the seller's advantage.

Information and Buyers' Behaviors

Information about the item for sale affects how aggressively or conservatively bidders behave. Bidders with inadequate information about the object for sale behave conservatively for fear of paying too much. The winning bidder, concerned about his lack of information, becomes susceptible to the winner's curse—"I won this auction because everyone else knows something about the object for sale that I don't know." When bidders believe they do not have all the information needed or believe that others have better information than they do, fear of what auction theory calls the winner's curse causes them to bid more conservatively.

The negative effect of the winner's curse on Large Companies is especially strong due to the very large uncertainties in valuing technologies and the high cost to do the experiments to reduce these uncertainties. The winner pays to acquire the technology, and then invests much more—animal testing, toxicology studies, human clinical trials-before finding out whether the technology can produce a successful commercial product or has no/limited value. Further, the valuation of life science technology depends on estimates of development, regulatory, and commercial factors, none of which can be known with any precision. The auction winner may find, after considerable additional spending, that the technology has no value or that the actual value is substantially lower than the value assumed at the time the technology was acquired. Without adequate or full information, potential buyers of life science technology may conclude that the risk of falling victim to the winner's curse is unacceptably high. These potential buyers will either withdraw from the auction or offer less attractive transaction terms for taking on the additional risk.

Eliminating the uncertainties and concerns about the winner's curse is not possible. Small Companies can reduce the effect of the winner's curse by providing complete information about their technology or waiting to begin the auction until important additional information becomes available. We will return to this issue in Chapter 14—The Best Time to Hold an Auction.

Avoiding the Winner's Curse—Case Study

An aggressively managed Small Company that focused on pain management was presented with an opportunity to acquire rights to a product that would expand its burgeoning pain management product portfolio. The product, for severe neuropathic pain, was about to enter Phase III clinical trials in the U.S. Phase III clinical trials done in Europe had demonstrated good results. The Small Company was concerned that regulatory and political issues would either make approval difficult or retard market acceptance should the product be approved.

Despite having a well deserved reputation for being aggressive in its business development activities, concerns about winner's curse were so strong that the company submitted a bid with minimal upfront and milestone payments. They decided that they would rather not acquire the product than have paid significant upfront and milestone payments and invested $30 million in clinical trials and then find the acquired product could not be commercialized.

How information is communicated influences whether potential buyers trust the seller. Trust in the quality and completeness of the information provided affects buyers' perceptions of risk. When buyers view a seller as trustworthy, their perceived risk goes down. Lower risk often yields higher selling prices. The relationship between trust and bidding is described in the literature as the classic lemon problem. The term classic lemon comes from the uncomfortable experience of buying a used car. Buyers assume that the used car salesperson is withholding negative information or overstating positive information about the car. Buyers, concerned that they may be buying a lemon, insist, or should insist, on a discount to reflect the value of what they believe to be the withheld information.

Whether the salesperson is or is not withholding information is irrelevant. What affects the price buyers are willing to pay (their bid) is their lack of trust in the salesman. The classic lemon problem accounts for why so many used-car dealerships have a name similar to "Honest John's Good-as-New Used Cars." Buyers believing that John is indeed honest will insist on less of a discount than those who remain skeptical.

Small Companies behave very much like "Honest John's" sales people when only the most positive technical and clinical information is presented. Expected time to commercial launch is less than minimal. Sales estimates are beyond stratospheric. Questions are not answered or answered partially. Large Companies have seen this all before. Having bought their share of lemons, Large Companies apply a large discount to the information or politely usher the Small Company off the premises.

How to Shoot Yourself in the Foot—Case Study

One of our clients was interested in acquiring a small cap public company. It was well known that the Small Company had been in discussions with others, and our client wanted to know whether there was time left for him to get involved. "We're well along in our discussions," the CEO told us over the phone. "We wouldn't consider stopping the process for anything less than a bid of $5/share."

The stock was trading in the range of $1.25/share. Our client's valued the company at $1.75/share. By telling us he expected $5/share, our and our client's trust in the CEO plummeted. We politely told the CEO why his estimates were grossly out of line. Seeing that his credibility was gone, he eventually agreed to consider our client's proposal of $1.75.

On the other side of the coin, information that is well communicated can create significant potential. A presentation by the Vice President for R&D of one of HVA's clients went a long way toward building trust with a Large Company considering acquiring a license to our client's technology. Questions were answered fully. There was no attempt to hide less than favorable clinical results. Additional work required for FDA approval was identified. Watching the reaction of the Large Company's staff, it was clear they were buying into the Vice President's view of the potential for his technology. The Large Company has undertaken a full-scale due diligence evaluation of our client's technology.

Information about the asset being sold plays an important role in attracting quality bidders to the auction. While intuitively obvious, auction theory proves that the expected selling price increases with the number of bidders. What may not be obvious is that the benefit of adding one or two additional bidders is greatest when the number of bidders is small. Having few potential buyers is the norm for life science business development transactions. In our experience, the number of Large Companies interested in acquiring a technology is almost never more than three or four, more often one or two. Using information to attract even one more potential buyer can have a substantial effect on the expected selling price.

Providing complete information about the object for sale benefits the seller in three ways: it reduces the drag from the winner's curse, it builds buyers' confidence in the honesty of the seller, and it attracts additional bidders to participate in the auction. Providing information can sometimes conflict with the need to protect valuable confidential information. Small Company management needs to weigh the benefits to the auction of disclosing more information and the potential harm to their company's well-being by disclosing more information. We will discuss how to resolve this conflict in more detail in Chapter 4.

Information About the Auction Status

Auction theory analyzes information about the auction itself as well as information about the object for sale. In an open auction, i.e., one where all the buyers are present, bidders observe who drops out and when. A bidder dropping out of an auction is bad news. First, a reduction in the number of bidders decreases the expected selling price. Second, valuation of the object for sale may decline when others observe a knowledgeable, wealthy bidder who stops participating in the auction. ("She knows something about the asset we don't know. We should be careful.") Of course, all but one bidder must eventually drop out. It is, however, to the seller's advantage to keep as many bidders as possible in the auction for as long as possible.

Potential buyers in sealed bid auctions, such as life science business development transactions, do not know who is in the auction and who has dropped out. Letting potential buyers know who remains in the auction benefits the seller. Ethical and legal considerations, such as terms of a confidentiality agreement under which the discussions between the large and small cap company are considered to be confidential information, place severe limits on what information the Small Company can disseminate about the state of the auction. In Chapter 5, we present some actual situations in which the Small Company lets potential buyers know, quite legitimately, about the state of the auction.

Auction Theory's Major Points for Small Companies

- What information the Small Company discloses about its technology and how the information is communicated affects the likely outcome of the "auction." The Small Company controls both.
- The number of Large Companies participating in the "auction" can affect the auction outcome. More, enthusiastic, wealthy are better than few, disinterested, poor. The number of auction participants and their level of enthusiasm reflect, in large part, the information provided by the Small Company.
- An auction benefits from more disclosure of information about the technology. Large Companies needing more information to support their buying decisions either withdraw from the "auction" or bid conservatively. Large Companies with sufficient information bid aggressively or at least less conservatively.
- By presenting positive and negative information and answering questions directly, the Small Company can win the trust of the Large Company. Buyers who believe the seller to be honest bid higher than buyers who believe otherwise.
- Buyers' behaviors change when the status of the "auction" changes. Ethical and legal considerations impose severe restrictions on the Small Company's ability to disseminate information about status of the "auction." Creative Small Companies find ways to avoid these restrictions legitimately and disseminate information that helps level the playing field.

Auction Theory and Leveling the Playing Field

Our intuitive analysis of how auctions work and the results of auction theory come together in their emphasis on the importance of information about the object for sale, the credibility of the seller, and about the auction itself. The remainder of *Leveling the Playing Field* describes how small companies can use information to best advantage in their business development efforts.

CHAPTER 5

SINGULAR ASSETS

How a singular asset increases the leveling power of an auction was covered in our previous discussion about auctions. A singular asset is a one-of-a-kind that provides significant benefits—financial, emotional—to its owner. Prices for singular assets are high because of the benefits they confer and because they are, by definition, rare. The same holds true for life science transactions when Large Companies perceive a Small Company's technology to be a singular asset. This chapter discusses what makes a Small Company's technology a singular asset as judged by a Large Company.

A technology is a singular asset when it meets two criteria from the point of view of the Large Company: the technology is superior to alternatives in terms of its potential to produce a product with a high return on investment, and the technology's IP creates high or insurmountable barriers for others developing a competitive product. A singular asset meeting both criteria has the potential to provide significant benefits to its owner because of its potential to yield a successful product and because its IP comes as close as possible to assuring that the technology is one-of-a-kind.

A technology meeting only one of the criteria falls short of being a singular asset. Clearly, a technology which is less attractive than the Large Company's alternatives is not going to yield significant financial benefits. On the other hand, weak IP means that the technology may not be one-of-a-kind. We also point out that weak IP encourages competition which in itself reduces the potential of the technology to yield significant financial benefits.

Examples of technologies that are singular assets are shown on the following table. All of these technologies have strong IP. Our analysis describes each technology's commercial potential, e.g., why it would be a Large Company's superior alternative.

Technologies that Are Singular Assets

Technology	Why Technology is a Singular Asset
Anti-obesity drug	Lowers incidence of nausea and greater weight loss; nausea is the leading cause of patients discontinuing use of competitive products.
Compression therapy device	Demonstrated ability to effect a clinically significant reduction in severe edema of the lower leg when standard compression therapy has been ineffective.
Intubation device	Reduces infection rates of intubated patients.
Pegylated liposomes	Extends half life of certain large molecule drugs thereby reducing dosing frequency. Technology has strong patent protection; there are no current alternatives.

Singular assets play an important role in the business development process described in this Guide. We will return to the subject frequently.

HOW TO
HAVE
A SUCCESSFUL
AUCTION

CHAPTER 6

FOUR ACTION ITEMS

From here on, the Guide focuses on the doing. We will continue to use auctions as our model because an auction is the best way for a Small Company to level the playing field.

Auction houses, of course, know everything we have been discussing; it is their business to get the highest price possible for their client, the seller. To create an auction that is most likely to yield the highest price, auction houses do the following.

(1) Assess, realistically, the value of the object for sale.

(2) Attract enthusiastic potential buyers who are likely to assign similar value to the object and have the means to pay for that value.

(3) Provide information about what is being sold, what makes the object valuable, the identity of other potential buyers (if possible), and the status of the auction

(4) Keep the bidding going for as long as possible.

Assessing the asset's worth enables the auction house to set a minimum bid. Setting a minimum bid sends the message that asset has value to the seller; the price has to be at least this value in order for the seller to be willing to part with the asset. Not setting a minimum bid sends the message that the seller will take "any reasonable offer."

Minimum bids allow for the possibility that the auction has failed to attracted the most desirable potential buyers. Should there be no bids above the minimum, the seller has the option to reopen the auction and attempt to find a better class of potential buyers.

The objective of the other three actions—attracting potential buyers, providing information about the asset, and keeping the bidding going as long as possible—is to create the level of competition most likely to result in a high selling price. An auction house invites potential buyers who are known to have a high level of interest in the object for sale. They provide information about the object to motivate these potential buyers to attend the auction and to allow the potential buyers to place the highest value on the object. As long as there is bidding or there is the possibility of another bid, the auction house, through the skills of the auctioneer, keeps the auction going as long as possible.

When the seller performs these actions, it has an important effect on the outcome of the auction. Value assessment, attracting potential buyers, and providing necessary information all take place prior to the opening of the auction.

> "… the auction game begins long before the auction itself."
> Paul Milgrom, *Putting Auction Theory to Work*

The auctioneer appears only at the beginning of the fourth step. Doing the first three actions well enables the auctioneer to do his job well. Imagine an auction where the seller doesn't know the value of what is being sold, few if any potential buyers show up, and those who do show up know little about what is being sold. Even the best auctioneer can do little under these circumstances. Now, imagine an auction where the seller knows the value of what is being sold, many wealthy potential buyers show up, and the buyers are enthusiastic about buying because they have a great deal of information. A mediocre auctioneer can get a good price; a great auctioneer can get a fantastic price. In the latter case, the auctioneer takes advantage of the competitive situation created by the first three actions to get the best selling price for the seller.

In life science business development transactions, the Small Company's negotiating team takes on a role similar to that of the auctioneer. The team's negotiating strength and the auctioneer's ability to get the best price come from the same source—how well the first three action items are done. Small Companies that complete successful business development transactions typically do a good job incorporating the four action items into their business development process.

In the following sections, we will discuss, in some detail, each of the four action items leading to a successful auction.

CHAPTER 7

ASSESS THE VALUE OF TECHNOLOGY

Sellers assess the value of what they are selling in virtually every transaction in commerce. By assessing value, the seller has some reasonable idea of whether a fair price is being offered (a minimum opening bid). Knowing value, the seller also knows how far negotiations can be pushed before putting the sale at risk (knowing when to keep an auction going and when to end it).

The number of Small Companies we see who do not assess the value of their technologies is far greater than those who do. The former companies do not know whether they are getting a fair price or how far to push negotiations. Large Companies assess what the technology is worth to them. As a consequence of Large Companies knowing the value of the technology and the Small Company not knowing, a frequent outcome is a transaction that provides considerably less value to the Small Company than the technology is worth.

Ignorance (of the Small Company) is Bliss *(for the Large Company)—Case Study*

A small cap drug delivery company with a new, unique adjuvant wanted a strategic partner who would incorporate the adjuvant into the partner's vaccines. An adjuvant can boost the effectiveness of a vaccine. Often, the effectiveness of a vaccine depends on finding the right adjuvant. With the right adjuvant, less vaccine per dose may be possible thereby reducing side effects. Large

Companies in the vaccine business compete aggressively to acquire adjuvants for their exclusive use that have demonstrated proof of concept.

The small Company's adjuvant worked well with two types of vaccines in pre-clinical animal studies. How well the adjuvant worked with other vaccines was not known. Successful animal studies are usually seen as demonstrating proof of concept.

Anxious to do a deal to fill a funding gap, the Small Company quickly entered into negotiations with a Large Company having a global position in vaccines. The Large Company proposed to acquire a license for the two tested products as well as an option to license the adjuvant for all their other vaccines including those in development. The cost of the additional licenses, should the Large Company exercise the license, would be a fraction of the cost of the first two licenses.

The Large Company justified its proposal by claiming that its upfront payment was large enough to acquire the license and the options. The Large Company had done a careful assessment of the value of the technology. Knowing the value of what it was acquiring, the Large Company's proposal was undoubtedly tilted quite steeply to its advantage.

Ignorant of the value of the license to the two tested vaccines and the value of the option, the Small Company could not determine whether or not the Large Company's proposed terms provided a fair share of the value of their adjuvant technology. Further, the Small Company lacked a rational basis to refute the Large Company's proposal or to make a counter offer. Knowing that Large Companies' initial proposals are often one sided, the Small Company asked for more. Concerned about jeopardizing the transaction, it hoped its request was modest.

Under pressure to do a transaction, with no idea of whether the transaction was fair, and with no ability to respond strongly, the Small Company accepted financial terms very close to the initial proposal.

Ignorant of the value of its technology, the Small Company likely fell far short of realizing the value it had created. Undoubtedly, the Large Company saw it had done a very favorable deal—as close to bliss as a Large Company gets.

Whole Pie Valuation

Being headquartered in New Jersey, the HVA team goes out for pizza weekly. Frequently, one of us arrives late for lunch. There are always some slices left for the late arrival. But how much of the order is the late arrival getting? Is he getting a fair share? Does two slices mean that he is getting a third? Not if we had ordered two pies. Not if two of us ordered four slices in total. And, not if we ordered an extra-large pie.

The Small Company in our previous case study found itself in the same position as our late-arriving associate. Terms proposed by the Large Company gave them some slice of the pie. Not knowing the size of the whole pie, i.e. the value of the adjuvant opportunity, this Small Company had no choice but to rely on the fairness of the Large Company.

Only by knowing the size of the whole pie can our late arrival know whether or not he is getting his fair share. Only by knowing the size of the opportunity created by its technology can the Small Company know whether or not it is getting its fair share. Measuring the size of a pie is, quite obviously, done before a slice or two has been removed. Analogously, the whole pie assessment of the value of an opportunity is done without regard to upfront payments, milestone payments, and royalties. Once the whole pie value of the technology is known, the Small Company can judge whether or not the Large Company's proposal provides the Small Company with an acceptable slice of the pie.

The following case study shows how whole pie valuation can affect the outcome of a negotiation.

Whole Pie Valuation—Case Study

In negotiating a medical device joint development agreement with a Small Company, a Large Company proposed upfront and milestone payments, an equal sharing of development and clinical expenses, and a 3% royalty on sales. The joint development agreement was expected to combine the Small Company's technology with one of the Large Company's products. The combination product, if successful, would address a major unmet clinical.

The Small Company did a whole pie evaluation showed that the project had a value of $200 million. The terms proposed by the Large Company gave the Small Company a $15 million (7.5%) slice. The value of the Small Company's technology and their paying for half the development and clinical costs suggested that something closer to a 50-50 split would be more appropriate. The Small Company submitted a counter-proposal which gave them a $100 million (50%) slice.

To make a long story short, the Large Company when confronted with the whole pie analysis had no choice but to agree that its proposal was one-sided. The parties went back to negotiations, refined the whole pie model, and ended up with a transaction whereby the Large Company got a $125 million slice. (The Small Company's valuation had omitted the value of some of the Large Company's IP.) The Small Company's whole pie analysis increased the value to them of the transaction from $15 million to $75 million.

Whole Pie analysis can also help a Small Company decide, before the start of negotiations, how to structure a transaction.

An Unexpected Surprise—Case Study

A Small Company's management determined that they would be satisfied if they could out-license their pharmaceutical technology for a $30 million upfront payment, a $10 million milestone payment upon regulatory approval to commercialize, and 12% royalty. The terms were based on management's review of what they saw as similar transactions. HVA did a whole pie analysis to check whether or not similar transactions provided good guidance for this transaction.

Our conservative whole pie valuation showed that what management had considered as satisfactory yielded a 10% slice of the pie. For transactions of the type being considered, a 20–30% slice is considered adequate. Management changed their target to a $35 million upfront payment, a $20 million milestone payment upon regulatory approval, and a 15% royalty on sales. The target would yield a 25% slice. At the time of this writing, we are negotiating a transaction that is almost certain to achieve management's revised targets. Without whole pie analysis, management would have likely settled for something less.

How big a slice should a Small Company expect? HVA has found that for most transactions the Small Company gets a 20–30% slice. 20–30% is an average from our experience. This is certainly not a hard and fast rule. How effectively the Small Company has created competition among potential buyers plus its negotiating skills affect how big a slice of the pie they get. The Small Company's slice is limited by the need of the Large Company to make an adequate return on its investment to acquire the technology, to develop a marketable product, and then to market the project. Calculation of the Large Company's return is beyond the scope of this Guide. A Small Company's CFO or transaction advisor can provide guidance.

Valuing Life Science Technology

Valuing life science technology is difficult; it is certainly doable. Financial investors (e.g., angels, VCs, funds) value life science technology regularly as part of their decisions whether or not to invest in Small Companies. Large Companies carefully assess the value of any life science technology they are considering acquiring. Small Companies, with more information about their technology than anyone else, should be able to value their own technologies as well.

There is no best or easy way to value technology. Public announcements of transactions similar to the transaction being considered can provide limited insights. Extrapolating terms and valuation from one transaction to another can be misleading, as we saw in the above case. Every transaction is unique. The size of the opportunity, the likelihood of developing a successful product, and strategic factors can vary widely among transactions that appear to be similar. Also, published transaction terms leave out much of the information needed to value the transaction. Following are excerpts from press releases announcing transactions between Small and Large Companies. Questions we would need to ask to value the transaction are in italics.

> **BOSTON (MarketWatch)—GlaxoSmithKline has signed a collaborative agreement to develop a new generation of therapies for inflammatory and autoimmune diseases that could garner partner ChemoCentryx up to $1.5 billion in payments**
> By _Val Brickates Kennedy_, _MarketWatch_
> _Last Update: 4:22 PM ET Aug 24, 2006_
>
> The companies will focus on developing therapies based on four chemokine and chemoattractant receptor targets.... The collaboration will also include ChemoCentryx's lead product, Traficet-EN, which is in Phase II/III development for inflammatory bowel disease, particularly Crohn's.... in addition to testing Traficet-EN for Crohn's, the companies hope to begin Phase II clinical trials within a year for ulcerative colitis and asthma.... the company sees filing to begin clinical trials for at least two of the three other drug targets by the end of 2007.

Terms call for GlaxoSmithKline to make a $63.5 million upfront payment to ... ChemoCentryx, ... in the form of cash and a Series D equity financing investment.

How much of the $63.5 million is in cash and how much is in equity investment? What percent ownership does GSK's equity investment get for its investment? What else, other than the projects included in the agreement, could affect the value of GSK's equity?

GlaxoSmithKline will also provide research funding for the project, with future payments ultimately reaching up to $1.5 billion if the products are successfully developed.
How much of the $1.5 billion is for milestone payments versus product development? What are the milestone triggering events? When are the milestone events expected to occur?

In addition, ChemoCentryx would be entitled to double-digit royalties on any products that make it to market and would be able to increase its royalty rate under certain conditions if the company agrees to co-fund clinical development through Phase III clinical trials. *Are the double digit royalties 10%, 12%, 20%? What would be the Small Company's spending on clinical development to increase its royalty rate? By how much would the royalty rate increase?*

Merck to Enter a Venture for Pain Drugs
By ANDREW POLLACK
Published: New York Times, March 20, 2006

Merck ... will enter a collaboration to develop new painkilling drugs with Neuromed <u>Pharmaceuticals</u>, a privately held biotechnology company.

... Merck will pay an initial $25 million to gain the exclusive rights to Neuromed's family of drugs for <u>chronic pain</u>. The most advanced of the drugs, NMED-160, has entered midstage clinical trials.

Merck would pay Neuromed an additional $202 million if NMED-160 wins approval worldwide. If NMED-160 is approved for a second use, and another drug is approved for two uses, payments would reach $450 million.

Are these milestone payments? Or, do these payments include R&D funding and royalties? What events trigger the milestone payments? When are these milestone events expected to occur? If the payments include royalties, what is the royalty rate?

The only useful valuation information one could get from either of these press releases is that Merck values Neuromed's technology at something above $25 million.

Discounted cash flow, despite its limitations, is the most widely used valuation methodology. Most Large Companies use discounted cash flow as part of their technology evaluation process. The fact that Large Companies use discounted cash flow should be motivation enough for a Small Company. Sharing a valuation methodology gives the parties a means to come to agreement on the value of the opportunity, to assess how a proposal would divide the pie, and then, as necessary, to negotiate inequities.

What makes discounted cash flow useful and, at the same time, difficult is that it relies on projections—how long to regulatory approval, how much money will be required to complete development and clinical trials, should a product get to market what sales and what profits will it generate. A discounted cash flow valuation is useful because it accounts for factors specific to the technology being valued. Forecasting the specific factors with any degree of precision is what makes discounted cash flow valuation difficult. (Information on discounted cash flow methodology can be found in any business school financial text book.)

Large Company Valuations

Large Companies assess the value of a technology very soon after there is a serious expression of interest by their scientists and engineers. First-pass projections of risk, development time, commercial potential, and marketing costs that underlie the valuation are based on company and industry norms. Though projections may be refined as more information becomes available, large deviations from industry and company norms are infrequent. Large Companies are reluctant to include the effect of large deviations from industry and company norms because their experience suggests otherwise. Projections based on significant deviations can cause the Large Company to overpay to acquire the technology. Factoring in significant deviations from norms require strong justification.

The use of industry and company norms is supported by Private Equity Industry Guidelines Group (PEIGG) in their March 2007, "Updated U.S. Private Equity Valuation Guidelines" which recommends, "The estimate of fair-value should incorporate all reasonably available information about the business and utilize assumptions market participants would normally use in their estimates of value." PEIGG is concerned with valuing private equity investments. Their advice is applicable in life science—fair-value is the most reasonable valuation of the technology; Large Companies are the market participants. (More information about PEIGG and the complete Guidelines can be found at www.peigg.org.)

Large Companies seek a balance between being overly optimistic and overly conservative. The valuation cannot be overly optimistic because Large Companies want to avoid overpaying. On the other hand, the valuation cannot be overly pessimistic to avoid under-bidding for a technology of importance. Given the challenges in making the projections that underlie technology valuations, finding the right balance can be a challenge. From our experience, the projections used by Large Companies to guide investment decisions are, on average, slightly more optimistic than conservative. Even so, Large Company valuations are, almost without exception, less than what the Small Company announces publicly.

Small Company Valuations

The Small Company's valuation of its technology should be done using the same approach as that used by Large Companies. At this stage, the valuation's sole purpose is to give the Small Company insight into whether a proposed transaction gives them a fair slice of the pie or if not, how far it is possible to push negotiations. Whether or not management chooses to share this valuation depends on the specifics of the negotiation. Small Companies should, like Large Companies, seek a balance between being overly conservative and overly optimistic and base their projections on industry norms unless there is a compelling reason based on the features that make the technology a singular asset. Small Companies should expect resistance from Large Companies on this point. Data-driven arguments are absolutely necessary to overcome this resistance.

Small Company's projections are almost always optimistic reflecting their optimism about there technology. A bit of optimism is fine. As illustrated in the following case study, overly optimistic projections can obstruct the business development process.

Separate Realties = No Transactions—Case Study

A Small Company developing a first-in-class pain management product routinely told investors the total market for this product was 1,000,000 patients. When the Small Company decided to find a strategic partner, its CEO wanted a transaction that valued the product based on the 1,000,000 patient potential.

Needing a strategic partner with regulatory and commercial experience with pain management products, the Small Company targeted Large Companies with an established presence in pain management. Several Large Companies submitted term sheets. All were well below the CEOs expectations. From what the Large Companies proposed, they were either looking for a bargain or they put a much lower valuation on the opportunity.

The Small Company's VP-Business Development followed up with the Large Companies. They indeed had a much different view of the valuation. Their valuations were based on their extensive experience in the market. For example, one Large Company expected that the planned Phase III clinical trials would, if successful, support usage of the product in a subgroup of patients numbering no more than 250,000.

Expanding the approved use to the larger patient population required additional clinical trials and long-term follow-up studies. Even if these additional activities were to be successful, the Small Company's product was unlikely to capture 100% of the market. (The leading competitor in this market has a 35% share.) This Large Company valued the technology based on an initial market of 250,000 patients expanding to a market of up to 650,000 patients depending on the results of future clinical trials.

Compared to the projections of the Small Company, the projections of the Large Company had lower market potential, increased cost to get to market, and higher risk (two rounds of clinical trials) for the product to achieve its potential. No wonder their valuations were much lower.

The frustrated CEO rejected what he considered to be low-ball offers. The Small Company's V.P—Business Development team has gone back to find a better deal. As yet, no transaction has been consummated.

Some readers may agree with the CEO's decision to reject what he saw as low-ball offers. We agree that a Small Company should not accept true low-ball offers. Whether or not the Large Companies in this case submitted low-ball offers is uncertain. Rather than turn down the offers, the Small Company might have confirmed industry norms for regulatory approval and potential market penetration and done a whole pie valuation. The Small Company would then be able to estimate the quality of the offers by estimating their slice of the pie from the proposed terms.

Technology Valuation and Singular Assets

Technology valuation should include a realistic effect of the factors that make their technology a singular asset. As we discussed in Chapter 4, a life science technology is a singular asset when it meets two criteria: the technology is superior to alternatives in terms of its potential to produce a successful product and the technology's IP creates high or insurmountable barriers for others developing a competitive product. Data should be analyzed carefully to decide how close a technology comes to meeting these two criteria. For example, a pre-clinical technology would have less data supporting its being the best alternative than would a technology with a product about to enter Phase III. Data on patents, issued vs filed, follows a similar pattern.

A technology may be the best alternative in terms of its ability to produce a successful product for several reasons. These include: a final product with significant therapeutic advantages over current and future competitive products, a faster, less expensive and more certain path to regulatory approval, and much easier distribution (e.g., a product that can be stored at room temperature compared to products requiring refrigeration. IP may take several forms as well. These include: the cost of working around the IP should the Large Company not acquire the technology and the advantage of delaying competitors' entries into the market. Valuations of the technology should reasonably reflect each of the above factors.

Due to the importance of valuing what makes a technology a singular asset, we will use two case studies for emphasis.

Rapid Market Penetration at a Premium Price—Case Study

Patients whose adrenal glands do not produce sufficient cortisol (adrenal insufficiency or AI) are faced with taking powerful immediate release corticosteroids (synthetic cortisol) for the remainder of their lives. World-wide there are no more than 300,000 AI patients. Regulators in the U.S. and E.U. see new AI products as candidates for orphan drug designation. Immediate release corticosteroids are only partially effective. Because immediate release products can not match the daily pattern with which a healthy adrenal gland produces cortisol, AI patients suffer from having too much or not enough steroids throughout the day. AI patients suffer from severe fatigue and a quality of life similar to patients with congestive heart failure.

A Small Company developed a patented drug delivery technology that allows corticosteroids to be delivered so as to closely match the daily production pattern of a healthy adrenal gland. It would seem that this would make the product using the drug delivery technology a singular asset. Large Companies evaluating the opportunity readily accepted this product's potential to gain market share rapidly when sold at the same price as the generic immediate release products. Not surprisingly, the returns on a branded product that had gone through extensive clinical trials, targeting a small patient population, and selling at generic pricing were unattractive. (The returns were, in fact, non-existent.) So while the Small Company's product was easily recognized as a singular asset, this fact alone added no value to it.

In order to assign value to the product, the Large Companies had to be convinced that the product could both gain significant market share and do so at a very large premium over generics. The Small Company, though short on cash, engaged an expensive consultant to do an extensive pricing study. The study focused on large payers and their policies towards reimbursing new drugs which competed with generics. Study results were sent out to the Large Companies which had previously signed confidential disclosure agreements. The pricing study, done by a recognized, independent industry expert, convinced several Large Companies that a large price premium was likely once the product demonstrated that it did improve quality of life for AI patients.

IP Protection Beyond Patents—Case Study

The entry of generic competitors, typically close to the date of expiration of the patents covering the technology, causes a sharp decline in a product's selling price and profitability. Royalty payments, consequently, are made only as long as the IP is in place.

Patents covering a Small Company's first-in-class product expire eight years following the date of expected commercialization. However, the Small Company's IP included closely held trade secrets for the production of the API (active pharmaceutical ingredient). A generics company wanting an alternate source would have to engage in a long-term and expensive development program even in the event the trade secrets were to be become public. The combination of the patents covering the technology and the trade secrets covering production of the API made the company's technology a singular asset. Whoever wanted to have access to the company's product and technology had to partner with them.

The Small Company worked hard to get the message across to potential partners. API production was highlighted in every presentation. Potential partners who submitted term sheets were invited to tour the API production facility.
The Small Company's hard work was successful. Royalties from its strategic partner will continue until there is a generic competitor on the market; certainly more than the eight years to patent expiration.

Large Companies are, understandably, skeptical about Small Companies' claims that a technology is a singular asset. Every Small Company makes this claim in one way or another; few support their claims with compelling, data-supported arguments. A compelling, data supported argument is one that would convince an independent panel of experts that the technology is indeed a singular asset, i.e., the product resulting from the technology would improve treatment or diagnosis, compared to competition, in a clinically important way. Small Companies should consider using their scientific advisory board, which is not quite an independent panel but close enough, to evaluate their arguments and suggest what additional information are needed to make their arguments more compelling.

Convincing a Large Company that a technology is a singular asset can have a very large effect on willingness of the Large Company to acquire the technology and at what price. The Small Company should therefore make considerable efforts towards this end. HVA has recommended to clients who lack sufficiently convincing arguments to defer their business development efforts until the data about their technology is more persuasive. Yes, it's that important.

Large Company—Specific Factors and Technology Valuation

Just as personal factors played a significant role in our Persian rug mini-case study, company-specific factors can play a significant role in how Large Companies value technology. Company-specific factors are characteristics which may make a technology more valuable to one company than to its competitors. These include the following:

- The product resulting from the technology fits the company's business strategy
- The technology fills a gap in the Large Company's portfolio of pipeline products
- The product will respond to real or perceived threats from competitors
- The product, if owned by competitors, would threaten one of the Large Company's market franchises
- The technology is well-understood by the Large Company.

The next two case studies demonstrate the power of including company-specific factors in the assessment of a technology's value.

Leveraging Company Specific Factors—Case Study

A Small Company developed a product technology with the potential to replace certain high priced, high margin specialty catheters used in the ICU. The Large Company, the world-wide market leader (65% share of market for catheters used in the ICU), had been aggressively pursuing the Small Company in an effort to acquire the technology behind the product. (Being pursued is a nice position for a Small Company.) Market leadership has advantages and creates vulnerabilities. In this case, acquiring the technology would be unlikely to result in significant additional market share for the Large Company. Should a competitor acquire the technology, however, the Large Company would likely lose a considerable market share and profit.

The Small Company CEO, at one time a senior executive of the Large Company, told his former employer he expected a proposal from them to reflect the competitive importance of his technology. He was confident that the Large Company's competitors would be more than pleased to acquire his technology. His insistence on leveraging company specific factors, here the Large Company's vulnerability, worked. The two parties came to terms more than satisfactory to the Small Company.

Knowing the company specific factors for each potential buyer can help the Small Company identify which potential buyer will put the highest value on its technology. Finding a potential buyer who, for whatever reasons, puts a much higher value on a singular asset can yield a very high selling price. For life science business development transactions, company specific factors are most likely to explain why one Large Company's valuation exceeds those of its competitors. The following case study demonstrates how this is done and its benefits.

PEGPharma Finding the Best Partner—Case Study

Hemophiliacs require approximately three doses per week of recombinant FactorVIII (rFVIII) to control their bleeding episodes. PEGPharma, an early-stage drug delivery company, had developed a pegylated liposome which when used with rFVIII, achieved bleeding control with once/week dosing. Commercialization of the combination product, or its equivalent, would represent a major advance in the treatment of hemophilia. Two small human clinical studies supported the safety and efficacy of pegylated rFVIII.

Lacking the necessary capital and expertise to bring a pegylated rFVIII to market, PEGPharma needed a strategic partner. Choices were limited to the three global manufacturers of rFVIII. Though there were no clinically significant differences among the rFVIII, being first to market and distribution strength had established ABC as a market leader with a 70% global market share. DEF had a 25% share and GHI a 5% share. After careful analysis, PEGPharma decided that the number two competitor, DEF, would value its technology higher than the other two suppliers. PEGPharma's conclusion was based on the following company specific factors.

- Among the three suppliers, rFVIII was most important to DEF. DEF had recently announced that accelerating the growth of its pharmaceutical business was their top priority. rFVIII was its largest healthcare product. rFVIII was much less important to ABC and GHI.
- DEF needed to gain rFVIII market share to meet its goals for the pharmaceutical business. A decline in market share would make maintaining the existing level of pharmaceutical sales difficult.
- Pegylated rFVIII would, upon receiving regulatory approval, be a major opportunity to gain share quickly. Without pegylated rFVIII, market share gains would come slowly if at all.
- Should ABC become the strategic partner, its resulting market share gains would come largely at the expense of DEF. In this eventuality, DEF would likely decide to sell off its pharmaceutical business.
- ABC would put a lower value on the technology since the sales of a pegylated rFVIII would simply replace sales of its existing product.
- GHI's small market share and weak distribution made it very unlikely that they would assign a high value to the technology.

PEGPharma approached all three suppliers. Efforts were focused on DEF. Presentations to DEF discussed the potential for market share gains and hinted at how much a PEGPharma/ABC partnership would adversely affect DEF's entire pharmaceutical business.

PEGPharma's analysis was correct. DEF was first to submit a term sheet and paid PEGPharma several million dollars to stop all discussions with its competitors. Knowing the importance of rFVIII to DEF, PEGPharma pushed hard during negotiations. Terms of the final transaction included a very substantial upfront payment, milestones in excess of $100 million, a double digit royalty, and funding for all future clinical developments in hemophilia.

CHAPTER 8

ATTRACT ENTHUSIASTIC POTENTIAL BUYERS

"Marketing a sale is often the biggest factor in its success."
Paul Milgrom, *Putting Auction Theory to Work*

Several potential buyers with similar high levels of enthusiasm and financial means competing to acquire a singular asset create an auction most likely to yield a high selling price. Getting the right potential buyers (those with enthusiasm and means) to participate in the auction is critical to its success.

While almost every large and medium sized life science company has the means to acquire a technology, only a few will have enough interest. A key part of the Small Company's business development efforts should be identifying these companies and then getting them to be enthusiastic participants in the auction.

Large Companies Asking for an Invitation

A phone call from a Large Company starting out with, "We'd like to meet with you to discuss your technology and how we might work together" is a Large Company asking for an invitation. The Small Company may not have begun their business development process when they receive this call. If so, business development starts when a meeting is scheduled.

HVA advises its clients to have these meetings. When a Large Company asks for an invitation, it has decided that there is, at least, a moderate interest in the

Small Company's technology. Welcoming the advances of a motivated buyer is good business.

An initial contact can lead to a transaction, either in the near future or down the road. Feed-back from the Large Company can help guide the Small Company's development efforts. By managing the information divulged, the Small Company can protect itself from Large Company's seeking nothing more than competitive intelligence.

Scientific and Industry Conferences

Small Companies can generate interest in their technologies by making presentations at scientific and industry conferences. Attendees at these conferences are interested in the topics under discussion. Large Companies send their scientists, clinicians, and engineers to these conferences when they have a strategic interest in the topics on the conference agenda. There is no other venue that offers the Small Company the opportunity to tell its story to so many of the right people.

The benefits of making presentations at scientific and industry conferences include:

- Presentations endorse the Small Company and its technology. To be on the program, the meeting's organizers have concluded that the Small Company has valid information of interest to those attending the meeting.
- Presentations address a powerful audience. Scientific and industry conferences are attended by scientists, clinicians, and engineers from Large Companies, often with the specific objective of finding new technologies.
- Presentations create opportunities to build and strengthen relationships with people at Large Companies most likely to be involved in a decision to acquire technology.
- Presentations build competition for "the auction." Conference attendees pay attention to who is taking notes during a presentation and who is having follow-up discussions with the Small Company's speaker.
- Presentation material can be used to provide information about the technology to potential buyers not at the meeting.

Attracting the Bear to the Honey
Presentations at Scientific Conferences—Case Study

PEGPharma's chief scientist (see case study on page 59 for background information) made regular presentations about PEGPharma's technology at major global drug delivery and hemophilia conferences. Senior scientists from all three suppliers of rFVIII attended these conferences. Two of the companies asked for invitations to the "auction". (In a three company industry, getting two to ask for an invitation is very good.)

The scientific presentations increased competition. The senior scientists at the three rFVIII manufacturers knew each other. They were aware of each other's presence at the conferences and which of them had follow-up conversations with PEGPharma. The pace of the "auction" accelerated noticeably following a presentation at which scientists from DEF, the acquirer of the technology, and one of its competitors had animated discussions with the PEGPharma scientists.

Presentations at scientific and industry conferences share many of the same benefits as articles in peer reviewed journals. Presentations have the overwhelming advantage of creating face-to-face personal contacts and in encouraging relationship building dialogues. It is not unusual for a Large Company's scientists, clinicians, or engineers to come back from a conference energized and excited about what they have seen and heard. An article in a peer reviewed journal rarely has the same effect.

Small Companies attending Large Company presentations at investor conferences may find the Large Company asking for invitations, though sometimes indirectly. Investor presentations often contain references to the company's business development strategies. Occasionally, as in the following case study, the Large Company is more direct.

Trolling for New Technologies—Case Study

At a recent investor conference, the CEO of Angiodynamics, a fast growing publicly traded medical device company, devoted part of his presentation to his company's external growth strategy. The CEO listed Angiodynamic's specific interests in vascular grafts, image-guided pain management, tumor management, and vascular access. All were new technologies most likely to come out of a university, teaching hospital or Small Company. Had there been Small Companies developing these technologies at this presentation, they could almost be assured that Angiodynamics would be an enthusiastic participant in their auctions.

Filling Out the "Auction" Invitation List

Not all Large Companies attend every science and industry conference. Attendees are not always diligent about reporting on interesting new opportunities. A Small Company cannot be at every investor conference. In order to fill out its invitation list, the Small Company needs to contact Large Companies directly.

Large Companies that have publicly expressed interest in the therapy targeted by the technology or in the technology itself make up the "A list." These are the Large Companies most likely to become potential buyers. Company websites provide for many Large Companies a detailed description of their technologies and therapeutic interests. The following, taken from Merck's website, shows how much information Large Companies make available.

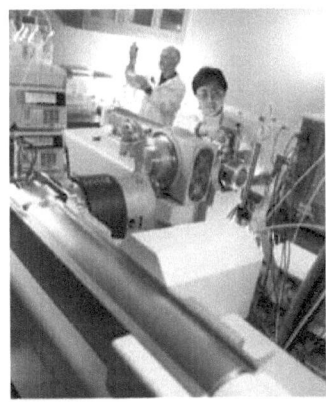

At Merck, our philosophy is to bring medical excellence to patients through first-in-class/best-in-class products. Our focus is on seeking alliances for New Chemical Entities (NCEs) and biologicals as product candidates for development. We are open to basic research collaborations and early research technologies, as well. We welcome partnerships that address unmet needs for patients, as well as technologies that will enhance the productivity of our research laboratories. Of particular interest are:

High Priority	Focused Interest
Alzheimer's disease	Antibiotics
Atherosclerosis	Antifungals
Cardiovascular disease	Antivirals (HCV and HIV)
Diabetes	Asthma
Novel vaccines	COPD
Obesity	Neurodegeneration
Oncology	Ophthalmology
Pain	Osteoporosis
Sleep disorders	Schizophrenia
	Stroke

Technology Platforms (Enabling Products and Improving Research Productivity)

Biologics and Antibodies
Drug Delivery
Information Technologies
In Vivo Imaging
Molecular Profiling
New Vaccine Technology
Research Technologies/Drug Discovery Platforms

Companies focused on therapeutic areas or disease states similar to that of the Small Company's technology go on the "B list." For example, a Large Company with a strategic interest in cancer became a potential buyer for a Small Company's technology to treat severe cancer pain.

Who Goes on What List—Case Study

A Small Medical device company was seeking a strategic partner for its implantable device to reduce high levels of fluid retention in kidney dialysis patients. The implantable device would be prescribed by a nephrologist and implanted by a vascular surgeon. The company organized its invitation list as shown below.

"A List": Companies providing implants and other devices for home dialysis. These companies have a strategic interest in dialysis, and they have relationships with nephrologists and vascular surgeons.

"B List": Companies providing grafts and catheters used for vascular access for patients on kidney dialysis. As with "A List" companies, these companies' products are implants, and these companies have a strategic interest in dialysis. Unlike the "A List" companies, these companies' relationships are primarily with vascular surgeons. Time and money would be required for these companies to expand their marketing and sales efforts to include nephrologists.

With invitation list in hand, the next step is deciding to whom the invitations should be sent. An invitation addressed to: "Large Company, Attention: Business Development Department" is unlikely to get a positive response. Doing this is similar to sending an invitation to a black-tie charity benefit to: "Owner or Current Occupant."

An invitation sent to: "Dr. L. Smith, Vice President—New Technologies, Large Company" has a far better chance of getting to someone who will give the invitation serious consideration. Should Dr. Smith know about the Small Company and its technology, or have a relationship with someone at the company, the invitation will be taken seriously. Having worked in business development and R&D for Large Companies, we know first-hand that no one can consider all the business development opportunities coming across his desk. We paid most attention to technologies we knew something about, largely from attending conferences, or from business and scientific colleagues whose judgment we valued.

Attracting potential buyers is best done through personal contacts and networking. As we have pointed out above, attending and presenting at scientific and industry meetings is an excellent way to build a network of scientists, clinicians, and engineers. Even when these people from the Large Companies do not initiate interest, they are much more likely to be responsive when approached by someone from a Small Company they have met. Contacts we made while attending a recent diabetes conference led to our finding three potential buyers for one of our clients who is developing a treatment for obesity.

No one in the life science industry has useful contacts at every Large Company. However, the industry is small enough that there are few degrees of separation between any two individuals. Useful contacts at Large Companies may very well know some of the same academics, clinicians, researchers, scientists, consultants, advisors and venture capitalists as the Small Company. Using a network to establish contacts is the next best thing to a direct relationship. Sending information over the transom should be a last resort.

With the invitation list in order, writing an invitation to attract large companies to attend the auction is the next part of the process and the subject of the next chapter.

CHAPTER 9

THE IMPORTANCE OF WELL-INFORMED POTENTIAL BUYERS

Information Creates Well-Informed Potential Buyers

Well-informed potential buyers are essential to having an effective auction; providing information is essential to creating well-informed potential buyers. Successful auctions disseminate two types of information to potential buyers: information about the asset being sold, and information about the status of the auction. Information about the asset being sold enhances the power of an auction by attracting potential buyers, contributing to their enthusiasm for acquiring the asset. Information supported by data about the asset being sold allows each potential buyer to place the highest possible value for the asset. Once the auction has started, information about the auction status increases competition.

Despite the fact that information benefits both parties in the transaction, the job of providing the information falls squarely on the shoulders of the seller. The seller in many cases (certainly the case in life science business development transactions) is the sole source of information essential to the buying decisions. When, as noted above, each potential buyer has access to the same information, the auction creates competition that benefits the seller. Conversely, failure to provide information is always to the seller's detriment. The value and importance of full disclosure of information are especially important when potential buyers perform extensive due diligence prior to transaction closing.

Occasionally, information does more than attract potential buyers and increase competition. The information is so overwhelming and forceful that a buyer makes a pre-emptive move. This, as shown in the following case study, can be of enormous advantage to the Small Company.

The San Francisco Earthquake—Case Study

A small medical device company located in the San Francisco Bay Area visited the headquarters of a Large Company to convince senior corporate officers to support in-licensing their technology. Though the Small Company had won over business unit support, the cost of the license and the spending required to develop the technology into a commercial product required approval from the highest levels of the Large Company's management.

The Small Company's presentation was attended by a Group President, the Corporate Medical Director, the CFO, and the VP—Business Development. The Small Company's excellent presentation, which lasted about an hour, discussed how its technology met an important unmet clinical need in a market of strategic importance to the Large Company and the financial rewards that in-licensing would bring to the Large Company. The presentation also covered the Small Company's development capabilities and IP.

Was the presentation effective? At the end of the meeting, while everyone from both companies was still in the conference room, the Group President turned to the VP—Business Development and said, "I want you on a plane to California Monday morning. Don't come back without a deal." That's an earthquake leveling the playing field.

It is worth noting that this Small Company went against our advice not to present financial projections. Here, the Small Company had enough confidence in their projections and their presentation skills that they took a chance and it worked. Had the V.P.—Business Development known more about the proposed therapy, the decision to present projections would have been a poor one. The Large Company eventually terminated discussions when the V.P.'s analysis identified several unsupported assumptions in the Small Company's projections.

Not all information causes an earthquake. Motivating a Large Company to participate in an auction is not quite an earthquake. It is a pretty good outcome nevertheless.

How the information is provided gives the seller a great opportunity to influence buyers' decisions. Art auction houses go to great expense to produce brochures displaying the items on sale to their best advantage. The brochures, in some instances, are so beautiful that they become collector pieces themselves. Art auction houses could provide the same information in black and white on newsprint at much lower cost. Art auction houses go to the trouble and expense of producing beautiful brochures because the auction houses have learned that the brochures have a positive effect on buyers. Small Companies can emulate successful art auction houses by providing information in such a way as to have a positive affect on Large Companies. This means the data should be presented in the most convincing way possible as well as anticipating and addressing likely objections.

Value Proposition

Small Companies become so enthusiastic about their technology that they may forget to link the information about their technology to how acquiring the technology would benefit the Large Company. The Small Company in our previous case study caused an earthquake in large part because they made the links and did so in a very convincing manner.

Sales people know that benefits, not features, affects buyers' behaviors. "Nobody buys a drill because they want a drill. People want a drill because they want to make holes" captures this. For life science technologies the equivalent statement might be, "No Large Company acquires technology because they want a technology. A Large Company acquires technology because they want a new, successful product." The value proposition describes how the technology could provide benefits to the Large Company buyer.

For example, a value proposition could describe how a product resulting from the technology would improve patient out-comes versus current therapies. Or a value proposition could describe how a product resulting from the technology would allow for a significant increase in the number of patients treated. Or a value proposition could describe how the product resulting from the technology would lower cost of patient treatment. The value proposition can describe multiple advantages should the Small Company's technology have this potential.

The value proposition translates the features that make a technology a singular asset into the benefits important to a Large Company. Hence, the benefits claimed must be well supported by the technologies' features. The benefit of improving patient outcomes can be made only when a technology has the unique potential to yield such a product. And of course, the Small Company's data must convince the Large Company that the technology is a singular asset for the Large Company to accept the value proposition.

Small Companies, believing the value proposition to be obvious, often omit it from the information provided to Large Companies. Our experience is that the Large Company may not automatically link features to benefits. When they do, nothing is lost by telling them again. When they don't, there is a great deal to gain by telling them.

Information—The Breakfast of Champions

Providing information can have the additional benefit of encouraging and supporting a well-respected senior scientist, engineer, or clinician at a Large Company to become a project champion. The value to a Small Company of having a project champion is enormous. Each of us has been involved with transactions which closed due mainly to the efforts of a project champion. It is not unusual for the efforts of a product champion to create a level of enthusiasm within the Large Company that manifests itself in the final transaction being attractive for the Small Company.

An individual takes on the role of project champion because she believes, despite reservations from her colleagues, that the Small Company's technology has enormous potential. A project champion becomes so enthusiastic about the technology that she will lead, oftentimes drive, the Large Company's decision making. Almost invariably, project champions are working against established interests or long-standing biases. They may go so far as to stake their careers and reputations on the potential for the Small Company's technology.

The project champion needs courage and must feel very, very comfortable with the Small Company's technology to take on this role. Comfort comes from understanding the technology, and the key to that comes only from information provided by the Small Company. The benefit of having a project champion is one of reasons we are emphatic about the Small Company being generous, perhaps more than they would like to be, in providing information.

A Project Champion at Work—Case Study

[We observed the following case study while working with the Small Company. Our knowledge of what went on inside the Large Company is limited.]

Senior scientists and clinicians of a Large Company listened politely to a Small Company's presentation about its drug delivery technology and positive results from pre-clinical animal studies. The technology, allowing patients to take the company's Type II diabetes drug once per day, could be of great strategic importance to the Large Company. However, as several of the senior scientists noted, similar drug delivery technologies had showed promise in animal studies only to have failed in Phase I human clinical trials due to a high frequency of unfavorable side effects and concerns about long-term efficacy. At the end of the presentation, the Small Company was told, "Thanks, but no thanks."

One of the Large Company's senior scientists thought the technology had enough potential to deserve further consideration. Earlier in her career, Martha Prindell, Ph.D., now Director of Discovery - Metabolic Diseases, had worked on some of the similar drug technologies which had failed in Phase I trials. She saw from the information in the presentation that the Small

Company may have solved the problems. Dr. Prindell became the project champion.

She knew human clinical studies would be the only way to produce the information needed to convince others at her Large Company. The Small Company lacked the financial resources to conduct even a small clinical trial. If a clinical trial were to take place, it would have to be paid for by the Large Company. The project champion had to convince upper management to fund a $5 million human clinical study in Eastern Europe.

Convincing the Small Company to work with her was less of a challenge. The CEO had worked successfully with a project champion when he was at his previous company. He arranged for Dr. Prindell to meet with the university professor who had developed the underlying science. Data from the Small Company's ongoing pre-clinical studies was provided as soon as it became available. The more information she got, the stronger her confidence in the technology's potential became.

As outside observers, we have only some of the details of what happened inside the Large Company. We know that Dr. Prindell gave several presentations to senior R&D and corporate decision makers. We know that there was a great deal of heated discussion, much of it behind closed doors. We heard, from others, that Dr. Prindell told the VP for R&D that she would resign if the proposed clinical trials were not successful. We do know that the Large Company agreed to finance the clinical trials.

The clinical trials succeeded beyond even the Small Company's expectations. A licensing/development agreement was signed shortly thereafter. Best of all, the drug delivery technology is expected to begin Phase III clinical trials 18 months ahead of schedule.

Potential Buyers' Information Needs

To do its job of creating well-informed potential buyers, information needs to be relevant to how potential buyers decide whether to attend an auction and what value to assign to the object for sale. Art auction houses, with decades of experience, provide information they know is important to their buyers. Auction catalogues provide details on the style of painting, the date of a painting, its condition, how it was stored, and proof of authenticity, all information that affect art collectors' buying decisions. Catalogues do not provide information about the molecular structure of the canvas behind the painting. Art collectors, even those who are chemists, have no use for this information.

More broadly, potential buyers need information to answer two questions: (1) Do I need to or want to buy the item being sold? and (2) How much am I willing to pay for it? Potential buyers' enthusiasm for participating in the auction and bidding aggressively depends on how well available information convinces them that they really want (or better yet need) the asset being sold. How high potential buyers will bid depends on how well available information allows them to assign maximum value to the asset being sold. This need presents an opportunity to the seller—provide the information that leads the potential buyer to answer the first question affirmatively and the second with a large number. To maximize revenue, the seller should take full advantage of this opportunity.

In the San Francisco Earthquake—Case Study, the information provided by the Small Company had the effect of getting the Large Company executive to conclude, perhaps prematurely, that it needed the technology.

Information and Large Companies' Technology Acquisition Decisions

How Large Companies make technology acquisition decisions was discussed in Chapter 2. We return to this critical topic again here taking the point of view of the Small Company providing information to support the Large Company's process. Many Small Companies underestimate the importance of information to the outcome of their auctions. Failing to provide sufficient relevant information may have several negative effects on the auction process.

- Large Companies may decide not to participate, which results in less competition
- Those Large Companies that do participate may assign low values to the technology assuming that the lack of sufficient information reflects considerable uncertainties about the technology's potential
- May create an overly long business development process since even those Large Companies who are interested will take additional time to get the information they need.

Large Companies are sophisticated buyers: they know their markets in great detail; they are keenly aware of major unmet clinical needs; they monitor their competitors closely. Their scientists, engineers, and clinicians read the pertinent journal articles, attend conferences, and follow patent office actions. Likewise, the marketing and sales groups have assessed the market as well as current and future competition. (Chances are high that a thorough market and competitive assessment was done much earlier as part of the Large Company's strategic planning process.) Once the Large Company decides to consider seriously a Small Company's technology, their people are well acquainted with public information. What is missing is information about the technology.

Providing What Potential Buyers Want—Case Study

Recently, we participated in a presentation by one of our clients to a large pharmaceutical company. The Large Company had an established presence in the therapeutic area addressed by our client's technology. A Confidential Disclosure Agreement had been executed prior to the presentation. Our client's presentation described the science, the clinical trials, and the path to regulatory approval. Commercial factors—size of the market, growth, competition—were not mentioned.

At the conclusion of the presentation, the Large Company's Vice President—Business Development thanked our client for presenting relevant information and for not wasting time on commercial factors. He later told us, "We know our markets extremely well. We find it a bit presumptuous for a start-up to tell us about our business. When start-up companies do this the market numbers are always outrageously high. We find it very difficult to complete a transaction with these companies."

Within a week, the Large Company began in depth due diligence as a prelude to submitting a term sheet.

When a Small Company's technology or its underlying science has not, as yet, been well accepted or is considered by academic and clinical experts to be unproven, providing relevant information is especially critical. The Small Company in this situation has the challenge of overcoming Large Companies' reluctance to make an investment in the new or unproven. One way to use information to deal with this challenge is demonstrated in the following case study.

Building Consensus for the New and Unproven—Case Study

Glucose control is critical to managing of Type II diabetes. Clinically accepted approaches to managing glucose work through peripheral organs. A new compound, developed by a Small Company, worked through metabolic regulation to control glucose. Large Companies in the diabetes business were skeptical even though the inventor was a recognized expert in diabetes and the compound had demonstrated efficacy in proof-of-concept animal studies.

A "second opinion" was needed to capture the Large Companies' interest. Large Companies in the diabetes business could have certainly consulted their clinical experts for a "second opinion." They did not bother to do so as is common in cases like this one. The onus was on the Small Company.

The inventor presented his concept and proof-of-concept clinical study at several scientific meetings. His presentations convinced opinion leaders that his approach and his compound did have potential. Several of these opinion leaders agreed to be principal investigators for the compound's clinical trials. Having opinion leaders agree to be principal investigators constituted a powerful "second opinion." Large Companies who had previously turned down the technology were now interested. A transaction was concluded with one of these.

How Much to Disclose, to Whom, and When

Many Small Companies decide to provide full information only at legal due diligence, the final step to transaction closing. This clearly has the benefit of providing important confidential information to the winner of the auction. The cost of this approach is the risk of getting a lower price for the sale their technology.

The purpose of legal due diligence is to assure that the Small Company has provided full and accurate information about its technology. Understandably, no Large Company wants to make a substantial commitment to a technology only to find that the patents are not valid or that the inventor has sued the Small Company over ownership of the technology. Legal due diligence often covers an in-depth review of the Small Company's experiments, pre-clinical studies, clinical studies, and communications with regulatory agencies, as well as IP documentation. Small Company's desire to restrict access to this information is certainly understandable.

Balancing conflicting interests makes the decision on where to draw the line on information disclosure difficult. Transaction contract terms impose severe penalties should the Small Company be found to have not disclosed relevant (negative) information. To get to an executed contract the Small Company can have no secrets, at least from its contractual partner to be. Why not disclose the information covered in the legal due diligence to all potential bidders? The seemingly obvious answer is that disclosing this information to all potential buyers, even under a confidentiality agreement, makes the Small Company vulnerable to the theft or misuse of the information. True enough. There is a very strong counter argument.

The counter argument rests on how Large Companies use information they find in legal due diligence. We have all seen situations where unfavorable information uncovered in due diligence results in the winning bidder asking to reduce the selling price or withdrawing the bid entirely. The Small Company, concerned about reopening the auction, finds itself now in a very weak negotiating position. When facing this dismal situation, the Small Company finds itself with few options other than giving the Large Company whatever it asks for to get the transaction closed. None of us, on the other hand, have ever seen a winning bidder increase its offer based on unexpected positive information discovered in due diligence. The Large Company has no motivation to do so and has every right to assume that all of the positive information was disclosed earlier. Information disclosed only to the winning bidder in due diligence can hurt but not help the Small Company.

Different potential buyers may assign different levels of importance to negative information; some potential buyers may not care at all. Making full disclosure to only the winning bidder assumes the winning bidder assigns the least importance to the negative information. Knowing whether or not this is the case is impossible. Further, full disclosure during the "auction" process removes the ability of the winning bidder to ask to renegotiate terms. The idea of full disclosure and supporting arguments were given to us by one of our small cap pharmaceutical company clients. We are obviously in agreement.

We are not, in any way, dismissing Small Companies' concerns about disclosing critical confidential information. Disclosing confidential information starts the next chapter. We are suggesting that Small Companies' executives balance the need to protect valuable information with the benefits of disclosing as much, (especially information that is less than positive), as possible. Small Companies should remember that the buyer is going to have access to all information, positive as well as negative, during due diligence.

CHAPTER 10

HOW TO CREATE WELL-INFORMED POTENTIAL BUYERS

Chapter 2 discussed how Large Companies use information in their technology acquisition decisions. We argued, hopefully persuasively, that these decisions were made largely on the scientific, clinical, and technical information provided by the Small Company. Potential buyers' behaviors, once they have made the decision to acquire, respond to information about the status of the auction. Most of this chapter is concerned with using the various types of information to create well-informed potential buyers. Scientific, clinical, and technical information of most value to the Large Company is virtual certain to be the information considered by the Small Company to be confidential. Disclosure of confidential information is, therefore, the first section of this chapter.

Disclosing Confidential Scientific and Technical Information

Disclosing scientific, experimental, and clinical information needed by the Large Company is problematic for Small Companies. They know, especially after reading Chapter 5, that Large Companies need this information to evaluate the technology and to assess its value. On the other hand, they are concerned that the Large Company will make unauthorized use of the information. Every Small Company has a horror story about a Large Company pirating its or other Small Companies' confidential information.

Anxiety is accentuated when the Large Company is known to be working on a technology similar to that of the Small Company's. Overlapping interests are common. The Large Companies most likely to become potential buyers are those with an interest in the therapeutic area addressed by the Small Company's technology (e.g., monoclonal antibodies in the treatment of cancer) or in a technology similar to the Small Company's technology (e.g. nasal drug delivery). Even with a Confidential Disclosure Agreement, in place some Small Companies are still reluctant to reveal confidential information. Reluctance to reveal confidential information can have fatal consequences in the Small Company's search for a strategic partner or licensee. The following case study is an extreme example.

Keeping Secrets—Killing a Transaction—Case Study

One of us, while working for a Large Company, suffered through a prolonged negotiation with a Small Company over terms of a Confidential Disclosure Agreement. The Small Company's technology was of great interest to the Large Company for which we worked; we and the legal staff had no choice but to get the Agreement done. The Small Company's CEO insisted that confidential information was his company's most important asset and that he needed "iron clad" protection. Under pressure from the business people and against the legal department's advice, the final Agreement conceded every contested point to the Small Company.

When the Agreement was finally executed, the long awaited package of confidential information arrived within a week. The package contained the Small Company's three published patents.

Assuming there had been a mistake, we called the Small Company's CEO. No, we were told, there was no mistake. We pointed out that the patent information, available on-line, could hardly be considered as confidential information. The CEO seemed surprised to learn that issued patents were public information. Remembering that our business people were really interested in his company's technology, we asked what we needed to do so that we could look at the Small Company's technical and clinical information. "We need a binding term sheet," the CEO replied. "We don't trust Large Companies until they put serious money on the table." "Even when we have a Confidential Disclosure Agreement with all the protection you asked for in place?" we naively responded. The CEO's "Yes!" ended the conversation.

Even the most enthusiastic of our business people gave up. They kept looking and eventually found another technology that met their needs. The Small Company went out of business six months later.

The following case study is a more positive example of the power of disclosing information even without a Confidential Disclosure Agreement in place.

From No! to Go!—Case Study

A small pharmaceutical company, one of our clients, insisted on providing very little information about its new, early-stage technology to treat metabolic disease in its Non-Confidential Executive Summary. The reluctance arose from a very bad experience disclosing information on another of its technologies several years earlier. So strong was the concern about limiting the amount of information disclosed, we were unable to convince our client otherwise.

We sent the Non-Confidential Executive Summary to Large Companies with an announced interest in metabolic disease. The few responses we got were tepid, at best. Conversations with colleagues at some of the Large Companies to whom we sent the Non-Confidential Executive Summary disclosed the problem. There was so little information about the technology that the companies' scientists could not evaluate it. The lack of data indicated that the technology was at too early a stage of development to be of interest. Saying "No" was easy.

We tried again to change the mind of the Small Company's President. Faced with the reality of how Large Companies make technology acquisition decisions, she agreed to provide more data in the Executive Summary, specifically data on the results of animal studies. Most Small Companies would consider these data to be confidential. This Small Company chose to disclose this data because disclosure was the only way to get Large Companies to become potential buyers and because disclosing the results of animal studies could not harm the Small Company.

Detailed information on the molecular structure of its compounds, the true source of the Small Company's concerns, was not included in the Non-Confidential Executive Summary. Large Companies did not need this information for this stage of their decision making process. Molecular structure information was critical to the Small Company and required thorough protection prior to disclosure.

Though the additional animal study data was far from comprehensive, it was enough to change some Nos! to Gos! Several Large Companies are now doing due diligence on the technology.

Small Companies' concerns about Large Companies' misuse of confidential information, though acutely felt, are not substantiated by the facts. Every Large Company we know of is very careful to respect the terms of Non-Disclosure Agreements. Large Companies developing similar technologies will insist that the Small Company limit its disclosures to avoid even the appearance of inappropriate use of the information.

A Large Company Limits Disclosure—Case Study

A Small Company with a technology to identify biomarkers for a specific disease engaged us to find a pharmaceutical company interested in using the biomarkers for drug development. The Confidential Presentation described several of the biomarkers identified by the technology.

After signing a Confidential Disclosure Agreement, we sent the Confidential Presentation to the Large Company's V.P. Business Development. Within two days of receiving the presentation, the V.P. Business Development called to request that the identified biomarkers, other than those previously publicly disclosed be removed from the presentation. He explained that his company was working in the same disease as our client and wanted to avoid even the perception of a violation of the Confidential Disclosure Agreement. Only when this information was removed would he send the presentation to his scientists for evaluation. He would accept the removed information when his company decided to move ahead.

Large Companies' growing dependence on Small Companies' innovations is further inducement for them to honor Confidential Disclosure Agreements. In an industry as small and as close knit as life science, news of bad behavior travels fast. We know of two pharmaceutical companies that several of our clients refuse to deal with because of allegations of previous misuse of confidential information.

Rational arguments do not always win the day. Whether they are comfortable or not, Small Company executives who want to have a revenue maximizing auction have little choice but to disclose confidential information. To do less jeopardizes the central role information plays in leveling the playing field. Disclosing more, rather than less, information builds interest and enthusiasm among potential buyers thereby strengthening the "leveling the playing field" benefits of an "auction."

Waiting to disclose confidential information until a Large Company displays serious interest certainly protects the Small Company. Unfortunately, waiting also deters the Large Company from ever making the decision to display serious interest. A Small Company reluctant to disclose sufficient information to support its auction would do better by waiting until it is more comfortable with its IP situation. Holding an auction without creating well-informed potential buyers is likely to produce very poor results, at best.

While disclosing highly confidential information is essential to create well-informed buyers, it should be done judiciously even when a Confidential Disclosure Agreement is in place. (If for no other reason than the executives of the Small Company can sleep at night.) Following are guidelines we have found to be useful in helping the Small Company manage the information flow.

- Before deciding to withhold information, the Small Company should be sure that the information is indeed confidential.
- Information should be considered as confidential when disclosure of the information could result in harm to the Small Company. In one of our previous case studies, the Small Company decided that there was virtually no likelihood that disclosing summary results of their animal studies could cause harm. On the other hand, information about its compound's molecular structure could.
- Information, which if disclosed, would hurt the Small Company's ability to secure patent protection should always be considered as confidential.
- To limit the possibility of a Large Company saying "No" because of incomplete information in a non-confidential information package, a Small Company should internally challenge aggressively every decision to withhold information.
- In responding to requests from a Large Company for additional confidential information, the Small Company should find out how the information will be used by the Large Company. Often, a Large Company asks for more information than its decision making process requires. The company that gave us the idea discussed in Chapter 5 about full disclosure gives potential partners only enough information to move them to the next step.
- Avoid Large Companies who are "tire kickers" or who have a reputation for being unreliable in respecting Confidential Disclosure Agreement. These are very likely to be the ones with whom any business relationship will be difficult.

Information About the Technology

Large Companies need four types of information about a technology: its feasibility and promise, how specific issues related to the technology will be resolved, what makes the technology a singular asset, and information about patents. We discuss information about feasibility and promise and information about specific issues here. Information about what makes a technology a singular asset and information about patents are discussed in the following two sections.

Information about feasibility and promise describes why and how the technology at its current stage of development is reasonably likely to become a successful commercial product in a reasonable period of time. In-vitro experiments, in the case of pharmaceuticals and vaccines, and table top models in the case of devices demonstrate feasibility and promise. Animal studies showing some safety and efficacy are a strong additional demonstration of feasibility and promise. Almost every Small Company provides this type of information. Those who do not provide this information usually find a lack of interest from Large Companies.

Information about specific issues related to new technologies becomes especially important when dealing with first-in-class compounds or new therapeutic modalities. Regulatory agencies become more diligent and require more data when faced with technologies new to them. The regulatory hurdles these technologies will encounter present significant risks (failure to get approval or requirements for extensive trials) to the Large Companies. Providing information about how to deal with these issues can reduce the level of risk the Large Company perceives. The following case study illustrates how one company addressed this.

GW Pharmaceuticals—SATIVEX®—Case Study

Note: GW Pharmaceuticals is a publicly traded company headquartered in the U.K. This case study was drawn entirely from GW Pharmaceuticals' website and press releases. Italics are the authors.'

From GW Pharmaceuticals' website:

"SATIVEX® is GW Pharmaceuticals' lead product for the treatment of severe pain. Phase III clinical studies conducted in Europe demonstrated SATIVEX® safety and efficacy in treating severe cancer and several types of neuropathic pain which had not responded to optimized opioid therapy."

SATIVEX®'s active ingredient is a purified extract of cannabis plant strains developed and grown by GW Pharmaceuticals. Negative publicity about "medical marijuana" created concerns that SATIVEX® would face "political" hurdles at the FDA and DEA in response to the source of SATIVEX®'s active ingredient. GW Pharmaceuticals chose to address these concerns upfront. Their non-confidential information package included the press release announcing FDA approval for their IND.

GW Pharmaceuticals plc, press release 4th January 2006

"FDA Accepts Investigational New Drug (IND) Application For Sativex®
Sativex® To Enter Directly Into Phase III Cancer Pain Trials in United States

GW Pharmaceuticals (AiM:GWP) today announced that the U.S. Food and Drug Administration (FDA) has accepted its Investigational New Drug (IND) Application for Sativex®, a cannabis-derived, oro-mucosal spray composed primarily of tetrahydrocannabinol (THC) and cannabidiol (CBD), a non-psychoactive cannabinoid, for the treatment of pain in patients with advanced cancer that has not been adequately relieved by opioid medications.

As part of this IND, the FDA has agreed that GW Pharmaceuticals may proceed directly into pivotal Phase III clinical trials in the United States in this very seriously ill patient population.

This IND follows a pre-IND/end of Phase II meeting held with the FDA in June 2005. The FDA has reviewed the extensive quality, safety and efficacy data generated by GW on Sativex in Europe."

This case study has a happy ending.

"GW Pharma signs U.S. partner for cannabis drug

LONDON, Feb 14 (Reuters)—Britain's GW Pharmaceuticals Plc said on Wednesday it had signed up privately-owned Otsuka Pharmaceuticals Co to develop and market its pioneering cannabis-based medicine Sativex in the United States. GW said it would receive total milestone payments of up to $273 million as well as royalties on future sales, and that Otsuka would pay for the U.S. development of Sativex as a treatnment for cancer pain and additional indications."

Information About What Makes a Technology a Singular Asset

Large Companies want more than a technology that "works"; they want a technology that "works better." Information about what makes a technology a singular asset is information showing how the technology "works better." What makes a technology a singular asset creates interest, enthusiasm, and drives the Large Company's valuation of that technology.

"Works better" is usually measured in terms of efficacy. For example, "our technology improves the survival rate of cancer patients," or "our technology reduces the incidence of post-operative infection." As reimbursement plays an increasing role in a product's commercial success, "works better" can also include why the product resulting from the technology will be reimbursed with attractive pricing. "Works better" can also be measured in terms of fewer or less consequential side effects, easier storage or transportation, or faster time to regulatory approval. However "works better" is determined, "works better" must be relevant to the potential buyers interest in and valuation of the technology. The Small Company should tie the unique characteristics of its technology with the best opportunities for a resulting product that "works better." The following case study illustrates this point.

Winning by Losing—Case Study

Currently available and soon-to-be approved drugs for the treatment of obesity are limited by the need to avoid side effects, such as nausea, and by patients becoming resistant to the drugs in 12 to 18 months. Nausea caused as many as one-third of obese patients to stop using these drugs within the first twelve months.

A small pharmaceutical development company was seeking a strategic partner to complete development and commercialize its new anti-obesity compounds. These compounds had been designed to minimize the above mentioned problems with the approved and soon-to-be approved products. Information about the product, the heart of the company's confidential presentation to potential strategic partners, was presented along the following outline.

Feasibility and Promise
>Underlying science
>Results from animal studies showing animals treated with the compounds had significantly lower food in-take
>Standard toxicology tests

What Makes the Technology a Singular Asset
>(Data supporting claims of less nausea and a longer period of efficacy.)
>Assay data showing company's compounds had better selectivity, oral bioavailability, and superior pharmacological profile compared to competitive products.
>Results from animal studies showing virtually no nausea even when the compounds were administered in high doses.

Breaking the data into two sections allowed the Small Company to highlight the much more important topic of the second section.

The link between what makes a technology a singular asset and how Large Companies assess technology is critical to the success of the Small Company's auction. Here the critical information are the data supporting claims that the technology is a singular asset. Scientists, engineers, and clinicians are by nature, by training, and by experience skeptical of any claim not well supported by data. Skepticism becomes especially acute when substantial sums of money and favored in-house programs are at stake.

Small Companies should be aware that scientists, engineers, and clinicians at Large Companies engage in often heated internal debates about how convincing data about a Small Company's technology is (as in our Project Champion Case Study).

These are not academic debates. Their outcomes have important consequences for the future of the Large Companies as well as for the future income of those engaged in the debate who own Large Company stock or stock options. The future of the Small Company and the future wealth of its investors and employees likewise depend on the outcomes of Large Companies' internal debates. No one from the Small Company will attend the debates. Data supporting the technology need to be persuasive; data are the Small Company's sole representative.

Information About Patents and Intellectual Property

Patents are intended to be a barrier to a third party copying the patent holder's ideas for that party's commercial benefit. Until a transaction is done, every potential buyer is a third party facing the barrier of the Small Company's patents. The Large Company acquiring rights to a Small Company's patents removes a barrier to its own development and now owns a barrier against others developing competitive products. For example, J&J's acquisition of the Palmaz-Schatz cardiovascular stent patent kept competitors out of the US market for several years. Conversely, by failing to acquire a Small Company's patent, or rights to a patent, the Large Company may find itself with increased risk (not being able to work around the patents) or cost (additional work to avoid the patents).

In-depth examination of patents is almost always left to legal due diligence. As we explained earlier, legal due diligence never works to the advantage of the Small Company. Nowhere is this more true than for patents. Patent due diligence serves the sole purpose of assuring the Large Company that the patents being acquired are valid. At this late stage, the opportunity for the Small Company to use information about patents to affect the Large Company's assessment of the technology's value is lost.

Each of these factors can, depending on the depth and strength of patent coverage, be highly consequential. Large Companies can assess the value of patents only by knowing the depth and strength of patent coverage; that is, the claims of the issued and filed patents. The value to a Large Company of a Small Company's patents comes from the following.

- The Large Company removes the risk of developing a product and then finding it violates the patents
- The cost and risk of trying to develop a technology that avoids the patents has been eliminated
- The Large Company's competitors face the costs and risks that the Large Company has avoided by acquiring the technology and its patents.

A list of patents included in Small Company's presentations falls far short of allowing Large Companies to make this assessment. There is a great deal of difference between knowing patents exist and knowing what they contain.

As with other sources of information, Small Companies have the responsibility of presenting information about patent coverage, even coverage information about issued patents. Large Companies never seem to spend any time looking at patent coverage prior to legal due diligence, or at least they don't admit to it. The Small Company, by providing information about patent coverage, can be sure that the Large Company considers patents in its valuation.

Information about patent depth and strength presented as part of the process of creating well-informed potential buyers does more than allow Large Companies to assess the value of the patents. Patent information presented early in the process motivates the Large Company to make this assessment. Having provided the information, the Small Company can certainly ask how the assessment of the patent value is reflected in a Large Company's proposal to acquire the technology.[1] Large Companies, aware that their competitors are getting the same information,

---

1   For example, the small cap company can ask what part of the upfront payment is due to the large global company not spending R&D dollars to work around the Small Company's IP.

may decide they have no choice but to value the patents in order to submit competitive proposals.

Patent information should, as far as possible, be included in the Confidential Executive Summary. Clearly, disclosure of confidential information and protecting pending future patent actions must be taken into account. Discussing the claims in issued patents, and some general statements about claims of future patent filings can almost always be accommodated. Patent information may be the single reason why someone at the Large Company decides to take a serious look at the technology. This is especially true when this information may result in the Large Company's internal program infringing one of the Small Company's claims.

Our arguments for disclosing patent information can be extended to other types of intellectual property, including trade secrets. The following case study illustrates how limited disclosure of trade-secrets can improve transaction terms for a Small Company.

Trading on Trade Secrets—Case Study

Royalties are typically paid as long as the acquired technology is covered by issued patents. The assumption is that once patents expire the market will be flooded by generic competition. The resulting decline in selling price makes paying a royalty no longer economically feasible.

Patents covering a small pharmaceutical company's technology would expire about eight years following product launch. In addition to the patents, the company had a library of trade secrets for manufacturing the key intermediate product. The Small Company was the only producer of this key intermediate. The company's patents provided broad coverage for the use of the intermediate.

Information about the Small Company's patent position was provided to potential buyers. Manufacturing experts were invited to the Small Company's manufacturing facility to verify the process. (The manufacturing trade secrets were not revealed.) The conclusion reached by potential partners was that any future competitor would have to undertake a long, difficult, and expensive process in order to produce the intermediate. A rather unattractive prospect for a low-cost generic manufacturer.

As a result, the Small Company asked for and got a transaction in which a double digit royalty would be paid as long as there was no generic competitor on the market. The royalty will likely to be paid for a good deal longer than the eight years left on the life of the patent.

We believe that, subject to having a Non-Disclosure Agreement in place, the patent information disclosed by the Small Company should be constrained only by potential limitations such disclosure would have on the Small Company's ability to strengthen its patent position.

Information About Markets

Despite what we said earlier about Large Companies knowing their markets, a Small Company whose technology has the potential to expand the market should provide information about how its technology will do this and by how much the market will be expanded. This type of information is especially important to Large Companies participating in static markets with an absence of recent technology innovation. These companies tend to view their market in terms of those patients who can be treated with current therapies. Other patients are not considered by them to be part of their market.

Expanding a Static Market—Case Study

HYDROBOOT was developed by one of our clients to treat patients suffering from venous stasis ulcers. Venous stasis ulcers affect as many as 2.5 million people in the United States. Compression bandages, the current gold standard, were developed in the 1890s, and there has been only moderate innovation since.

1.25 million venous stasis ulcer patients, about half of those with the condition, are treated with compression bandages; the other 1.25 million do not seek treatment. Of those seeking treatment, 500—600,000 discontinue treatment because compression bandages were ineffective or because of the discomfort of compression bandages. Concern about discomfort is one of the many reasons so many patients do not seek treatment at all. So the market for compression bandages covers no more than half of those with the condition.

A pilot clinical trial comparing HYDROBOOT to compression bandages showed HYDROBOOT improved patient compliance significantly due to greater comfort. It appeared to be as effective in treating de-novo patients as compression bandages and to be effective for patients whose ulcers had not responded to standard compression therapy.

HYDROBOOT was looking for a Large Company to market the product. To attract companies (most of which are selling compression bandages) to its "auction," HYDROBOOT provided information that the potential patient population was 25–50% larger (considering patients who had discontinued therapy and attracting patients who are not now in therapy) and that there was no competition for these patients.

There are few technologies that create new markets or expand existing markets. More often, a technology offers the potential to gain share in an existing market, either by replacing current products or by allowing a higher selling price than existing products. Small Companies believing their technology can create new markets or expand existing markets need to make very convincing arguments to persuade skeptical Large Companies.

Information about the Status of the Auction

The Small Company has limited ability to communicate information to auction participants about who else is bidding or how much they are bidding. Providing this information may violate terms of a Confidential Disclosure Agreement and is certainly unethical. By being creative the Small Company can provide some information ethically.

Scientific, clinical, and industry meetings can be used by Small Companies to give Large Companies a pretty good idea about who is on their potential buyer list. Another approach is illustrated below.

A Shopping Trip to Build Competition—Case Study

A European start-up developing a product to improve outcomes for patients on intubators attracted interest through its presentation at a new medical technology conference. Business development people from all the Large Companies in the intubator market were present at the meeting, attended the follow-up session, and made further contact with the company during the meeting.

One of the companies moved very quickly to sign a confidentiality agreement. A month or so after the conference, the start-up's CEO came to the U.S. to give the interested party a presentation of confidential information. At HVA's suggestion, he also arranged for less formal meetings with the other companies who had shown interest. In scheduling each meeting, the CEO told his hosts that he had other meetings in U.S with interested parties. (The CEO paid for his own travel expenses.)

Because letting potential buyers know that others are in the auction is so important and is rarely done well, we will add one more case study.

Dropping a Big Hint—Case Study

One of us, when working for a Large Company, attended an industry conference at which we had scheduled an afternoon meeting with a Small Company to discuss licensing one of its technologies. To confirm the appointment, we walked over to the Small Company's exhibition booth just prior to noon. On the way over, we saw the president of the Small Company and Leon Hirsch, at the time the CEO of U.S. Surgical, one of our large competitors, on their way out to lunch. The president made a special point of saying hello. There was no doubt this was not an accident. And, there was no doubt, in our minds, about the identity of one of the other potential buyers or his level of interest. Of course, Mr. Hirsch saw us and got a similar message.

We can only guess whether this less than subtle tactic caused U.S. Surgical to close a transaction with this Small Company soon after or how much it influenced U.S. Surgical to pay considerably more than we were prepared to offer.

Providing information on bids or levels of interest is much more difficult. It is certainly unethical for a Small Company to provide details of a Large Company's bid or level of interest. We believe it is ethical to tell one potential buyer that an offer from another buyer is in hand or to tell one potential buyer that her bid is less attractive than a bid already received. Canceling a negotiating session or terminating negotiations can also signal to the Large Company that there is a higher bid on the table.

CHAPTER 11

KEEP THE AUCTION GOING
AS LONG AS POSSIBLE

"Going...., going...., going....,gone." Experienced auctioneers know they can get the highest selling price by giving potential buyers enough time to decide whether or not to bid, recognizing when the bidding has stopped and bringing down the gavel. Ending the auction is very important for Small Companies. Knowing when to end is much more difficult.

The Small Company's Dilemma

Large Companies, after taking several months to submit a term sheet, expect a prompt response from the Small Company. They are not shy about pressuring a Small Company for a response. Some of the desire for a prompt response comes from the Large Company's senior executives who, having approved the term sheet, need to know whether or not they should include the Small Company's technology in their plans. Most of the pressure for a response expresses the Large Company's desire to cut short the auction. Large Companies are well aware of how auctions work to the advantage of the Small Company.

Time pressure would be less troublesome if the Small Company had two or more Large Companies submitting term sheets at the same time. The Small Company can then compare term sheets and ask for better terms where appropriate. Receiving two or more term sheets at the same time happens infrequently. The Small Company most often responds without knowing whether another term sheet will be forthcoming and if so, what it will contain. The following case study illustrates this point.

Dropping the Ball at the Goal Line—Case Study

A Large Company had begun serious negotiations to acquire a Small Company. The Small Company's primary asset was a technology critical for the Large Company's publicly announced strategy. With verbal approval from its CEO, the Large Company's business development team submitted a term sheet. Proposed terms included providing bridge financing so that the Small Company could cancel its next round of fund raising. Proposed terms, the bridge financing, and the CEO's verbal approval were sufficiently attractive for the Small Company to stop its auction and cancel its fund raising activities. The Small Company knew that the Large Company could move to a final contract only with approval from its Board of Directors. As far back as any one could remember, the Board had approved every one of the CEO's acquisition requests. A session to begin negotiating contract terms was scheduled two days after the Large Company's Board of Directors meeting.

The night before the Board Meeting, the Large Company's negotiating team was informed that the transaction had been pulled off the Board agenda. The CEO no longer supported the transaction. Earlier that day, one of the Large Company's businesses, one not involved with the acquisition, announced it would miss its quarterly earnings target by a wide margin. The size of the earnings miss combined with the costs of the proposed transaction would cause the Large Company to fall short of the annual earnings estimates provided to investors. The CEO decided that maintaining credibility with investors was more important than going ahead with the transaction.

Executives of the Small Company were irate when they found out there was to be no transaction. They did manage to get enough money from existing investors to keep the company going. Fortunately for the Small Company, it was acquired within a year at a price substantially higher than what had been offered by the Large Company.

The point of this case study is not that Large Companies are untrustworthy. The Large Company, up until the day before the Board meeting, operated in good faith. Our point is that decisions at Large Companies, affected by a myriad of factors, are not possible to predict, especially for those on the outside.

Positive events are equally difficult to predict as shown in examples from our experience.

- A Large Company that did not return phone calls or emails for several months re-entered the auction as an enthusiastic potential buyer. A strong supporter of the technology was promoted to a senior level position.
- In a similar case, a Large Company that had told us they were not interested in our client's technology, reentered the auction when an issue that had previously diverted their attention was resolved much sooner than expected.
- A Large Company with no known prior interest in pain therapy expressed serious interest in the pain therapy technology of one of our clients. The Business Development Director explained that his company had recently made an as yet unpublicized strategic decision to enter the pain market and were pursuing aggressively the type of technology offered by our client.

With no way to anticipate the future behavior of potential bidders, how does the Small Company know when to gavel the auction to a close? Bringing down the gavel too quickly shuts off the possibility of more attractive terms coming in later from another Large Company.

On the other hand, waiting to bring down the gavel presents different problems. Waiting sends a negative message to the Large Company that its proposed terms are far below expectations or that its proposed terms will be used as leverage with other Large Companies. The Large Company may pull its term sheet off the table as a consequence. Or, the Large Company may decide to pull its bid off the table and pursue other opportunities where it sees another transaction more likely to close. Should the Large Company pull its bid off the table, the Small Company faces the uncertainty of whether or not other Large Companies will submit attractive term sheets or whether there will be any additional terms sheets at all.

When subsequent term sheets are less attractive, the Small Company must either accept less attractive terms or go back to the first Large Company. That Large Company may no longer be interested. If still interested, the Large Company's subsequent offer will very likely be less attractive than what was offered initially. The Small Company's situation is even worse when the rejected term sheet is the only one it receives. Here, its choices are not selling its technology or going back to the one company, hat in hand.

The Small Company can decide to defer a decision about accepting a term sheet and begin negotiations while waiting for other, hopefully more attractive, term sheets from others. This tactic is, at best, a short-term fix. Shortly after negotiations begin, the Large Company will try to end the auction by asking for an exclusivity agreement as a condition to continue negotiations. Under an exclusivity agreement, the Small Company agrees to negotiate exclusively with one Large Company for a specified period of time. Exclusivity agreements are discussed in some detail later in this chapter.

Accepting the exclusivity agreement effectively makes the Large Company the sole potential buyer for at least as long as the exclusivity agreement is in effect. If the Small Company refuses to enter into an exclusivity agreement, the Large Company may very well decide not to continue negotiations. Having to decide whether or not to accept each term sheet sequentially is the Small Company's dilemma. How to resolve the dilemma is discussed below.

Resolving the Dilemma

The Small Company should begin negotiations with the first Large Company that submits a satisfactory term sheet unless there is a very high likelihood of other term sheets being submitted in the immediate future. A satisfactory offer has three attributes: (1) the value of the offer compares favorably with the Small Company's valuation of its technology, (2) the structure of the proposed transaction (upfront payments, milestone payments and royalties) meets the Small Company's objectives, and (3) the Large Company is a desirable buyer. A Large Company is a desirable buyer when it has the will and capability to complete the transaction and to develop the technology so long as it makes sense to do so. A significant amount of the Small Company's return from selling its technology will most likely come from milestone payments as the project nears regulatory approval to commercialize and from royalties on the commercialized product. As a result, the benefits of selecting a desirable buyer can be substantial. Chapter 14 discusses selecting a desirable buyer.

Starting negotiations with the Large Company that submits the first satisfactory offer may seem to some an overly conservative approach. (Starting negotiations with a Large Company is very different from agreeing to negotiate with only that company, i.e., having an exclusivity agreement.) Uncertainty about the prospective behavior of other Large Companies combined with the Small Company's weakened negotiating position should it lose what turns out to be its best or only satisfactory bid justifies taking a conservative stance on this issue.

And If the Offer is Not Satisfactory?

When the first term sheet falls far short of the Small Company's expectations, the Small Company has to have confidence in the value of its technology and confidence that the auction will yield a satisfactory bid. Here, the Small Company is following the example of auction houses that will not sell a work of art for less than a pre-determined opening price. There is one exception. Sellers under pressure to close the sale have less leeway to wait for the auction process to work. Sellers under pressure are the subject of the final section of this chapter.

When a term sheet is unsatisfactory, responding along the following lines is appropriate, "Thank you for your term sheet. We are discussing this opportunity with others, and we are not yet ready to move to serious negotiations with you or any of the other potential buyers. When we are ready to enter negotiations, we expect to do so with other parties whose terms are more attractive than what you've proposed. Should you decide to revise your term sheet, we would be pleased to consider it." A statement like this informs the Large Company that there is an auction, that the Small Company has confidence in the auction process, the Small Company is not having a "fire sale," and that the Large Company can continue to participate in the auction should it choose to do so.

Large Companies' opening bids are almost never their best offers. In hopes of picking up a bargain from a Small Company that does not know the value of its technology or is under pressure to sell, the opening bid may be surprisingly low.

Telling the Large Company that it is in a competitive auction can motivate it to offer better terms. Some may drop out of the auction at this point. As their offers fail to meet the Small Company's criteria, their loss is not of consequence.

Exclusivity Agreements

Exclusivity agreements are a way for a Large Company to shut down an auction. Under terms of the exclusivity agreement, the Small Company agrees to cease all contacts with other potential buyers and negotiate only with the Large Company for a specified period. For that period, the Large Company is the only potential buyer.

Exclusivity agreements are one-sided. The Small Company can negotiate exclusively with the Large Company. The Large Company can continue to develop its own technology, look for and evaluate other technologies, and negotiate with other parties. To our knowledge, a Large Company has never agreed to reciprocal terms. An exclusivity agreement is analogous to an auctioneer stopping the bidding to allow the leading bidder to take a closer look at the item for sale. The leading bidder has the prerogative to buy the asset at the price of his last bid or walk away with no further obligation. No professional auctioneer would ever allow this.

A Large Company may justify its request for an exclusivity agreement by arguing they are making a considerable investment—the cost of the evaluation— with some risk that their evaluation is negative and the additional risk of a positive evaluation only to find one of its competitors has acquired the technology. While there is some truth in these arguments, the Large Company's primary motivation is to end the auction as early as possible. And, a Small Company that accepts an exclusivity agreement early in the negotiating process send a very strong signal that there are few, if any, other potential buyers.

Exclusivity agreements create value for the Large Companies. This value depends largely on the length of the exclusivity period, the value of the technology, and the likelihood the Large Company will acquire the technology at the end of the exclusivity period.

- The longer the exclusivity period, the more difficult it will be for the Small Company to restart its auction.

- The higher the value of a technology the more likely that other Large Companies will be interested.
- The more likely the Large Company is to acquire the technology the more important it is that the technology remains available.

The Small Company should avoid exclusivity agreements to the extent possible. When a Small Company does agree to an exclusivity agreement, it should recognize that the agreement has value for the Large Company and insist on compensation. Compensation provides some assurance that the Large Company has a serious intent to acquire the technology because compensation usually requires approval from a senior level corporate executive.

The amount of compensation is a matter of negotiation. There are no easy formulae. We advise our clients that the amount of compensation should be enough that the Large Company would have to think twice before walking away from negotiations.

Like so much else, the ability of the Small Company to turn down requests for an exclusivity agreement or to negotiate adequate compensation upon acceptance, depends upon how strongly the Large Company wants the technology, believes the technology is a singular asset, and is concerned about others bidding for the technology.

Pre-Emptive Proposals

A pre-emptive proposal, where a Large Company submits a terms sheet with very, very attractive terms, is another tactic to end the auction prematurely. The Small Company has a limited time (usually a week) to accept the proposal and sign an exclusivity agreement, otherwise the proposal is withdrawn. Pre-emptive proposals, though putting a great deal of pressure on the Small Company, may be a very good deal, or not.

A pre-emptive proposal may signal that the Large Company considers acquiring the technology to be of great strategic importance. The Large Company, by revealing its intent, has gone a long way towards leveling the playing field. (Pre-emptive proposals do not arise out of nowhere. Receiving a pre-emptive proposal usually means that the Small Company has done a great job creating well-informed potential buyers and communicating a compelling case as to why its technology is a singular asset.)

Or, some Large Companies use a pre-emptive proposal to end the auction and then find reasons (often during due diligence) to reduce their proposed terms significantly. As we have seen, once the Small Company ends the auction it has lost a great deal of negotiating strength.

How does a Small Company tell the difference between a serious preemptive offer and one intended to weaken the Small Company's negotiating strength? We suggest using a response very similar to the one we suggested using for an inadequate term sheet; "Thank you for your term sheet. We are discussing this opportunity with others, and we are not yet ready to move to serious negotiations with you or any of the other potential buyers. Should you decide to revise your term sheet, we would be pleased to consider it." This differs from the response to an unsatisfactory proposal; it leaves out, "When we are ready to enter negotiations, we expect to do so with other parties whose terms are more attractive than what you've proposed." The intent is determining the sincerity of Large Company's pre-emptive proposal.

A Large Company whose pre-emptive bid is sincere may very well decide to increase their bid when they are convinced the Small Company has alternatives. In any event, a Large Company with serious interest in the technology will not walk away from the auction. A Large Company that, at this point, walks away did not have a serious interest in the technology to begin with.

In response to a preemptive proposal, a Small Company may try to get other Large Companies to accelerate their review of the Small Company's technology and submit term sheets. We have found it extremely difficult to get any Large Company to accelerate their technology review process. The Small Company does not have much to lose by using this tactic. It should be realistic and realize that its chance of success is quite small.

While the Small Company should exercise caution before accepting a pre-emptive proposal, there is no reason to turn down an acceptable offer just because it comes in at the beginning of the auction process. A Small Company should accept a pre-emptive proposal only when: the proposed terms are much better than could be expected, factors which support the Large Company putting a high bid on the table are well-understood, the Large Company has verified that their pre-emptive bid has approval by a senior corporate executive, the Small Company management believes that the final transaction will have terms close to what is in the preemptive offer, and the Large Company is a desirable buyer.

Under Pressure

In the opening of this chapter, we discussed how pressure from Large Companies can adversely affect the outcome of a Small Company's auction. Pressure can come from inside the Small Company as well. Investors' desires to close a deal quickly to validate the technology or to support an IPO, and the Small Company's need for a non-dilutive infusion of cash creates significant pressure to get a transaction done as quickly as possible. A Small Company in this situation might accept the first reasonable, but not necessarily satisfactory, offer. When a seller has to accept a less than satisfactory offer, the benefits of holding an auction are reduced significantly.

Large Company business development executives love finding an opportunity to acquire technology from a Small Company under pressure to close a transaction quickly. The Large Company that has submitted the first reasonable offer is now the only potential buyer. Other Large Companies, that might have offered better terms, quickly become aware the auction has stopped. Their calls and emails are returned slowly, if at all; requests for meetings are deferred to some indefinite time in the future. Most lose interest in the technology assuming a transaction will be closed shortly. Everyone knows that should the auction restart something must be wrong with the technology or with the Small Company itself.

An auction for what potential buyers believe to be damaged goods is unlikely to yield even a reasonable selling price. With no alternatives other than restarting an auction with what is viewed as damaged goods, the pressurized Small Company has little negotiating strength. The playing field has been tilted up almost straight up to the advantage of the Large Company.

Small Companies would do well to avoid finding themselves in pressure situations. Sometimes this is unavoidable. Even here, the Small Company should behave as if it is conducting an auction process. The appearance of competition is better than no competition at all. The Small Company should do everything it can to have viable alternatives to accepting any offer that surface.

THE AUCTION
AND
THE SMALL
COMPANY

CHAPTER 12

WHAT IF?

We asked friends and colleagues for comments as we prepared this Guide. The issues they raised most often were: "What if the technology does not have substantial value?" "What if no one shows up for the "auction?" and "What if there is only one potential buyer?" Each scenario is discussed below.

What If the Technology Does Not Have Substantial Value?

If indeed the technology has very limited value—minimal patent protection, likely infringement of existing patents held by others, no advantages versus competing technologies, difficult manufacturing—we doubt that having an auction is worth the effort. The Small Company may decide to try an auction rather than abandon their technology. Though they may get lucky, the chances of success are not great.

What If No One Shows Up for the Auction?

Having no one show up or having no one submit a satisfactory proposal is a difficult and disheartening situation. An absence of potential buyers indicates a serious, but not necessarily fatal, problem. The Small Company needs to make a serious effort to diagnose why this happened and respond accordingly.

No Potential Buyers—Diagnosis and Response

Reason Why No One Shows Up	**Small Company Response**
Technology may have value to someone not on the original invitation list.	Cast a wider net to attract new potential buyers; consider Large Companies working on similar technologies or closely related therapeutic targets.
Technology may have value in applications, indications, or patient populations different from what was originally intended.	Consider making additional investments to prove technology has value in these applications, indications, or patient populations.
The "auction" was held too early before technology had demonstrated significant value.	Consider making additional investments to advance technology closer to proof-of-principle.
IP strength limited or unclear	File IP or improve filings.

Following are two case studies demonstrating how two Small Companies responded to no one showing up to their auctions.

Good News From Unexpected Places—Case Study

Xrex had developed a unique therapeutic approach to treating a rare, but severe, chronic, metabolic condition. With 200,000 patients world-wide and existing treatment options having limited efficacy, European and U.S. regulatory agencies gave Xrex's technology orphan drug designation. Xrex's disease target was treated by a few endocrinologists. Xrex targeted specialty drug companies, especially those with an endocrinology focus. (The market was too small to be of interest to the major drug companies.) None went beyond looking at the Non-Confidential Executive Summary.

Xrex diagnosis of why no one showed up at their auction revealed that the market for their technology was too small even for specialty drug companies. They reopened their auction targeting smaller companies that had a product in late stages of development for which Xrex's product would be complementary (i.e., both products would be sold to the same small group of prescribing physicians). Two companies from Xrex's second set of targets stepped forward. The first was a company with a newly launched product used by endocrinologists and one unrelated medical specialty. The second company specialized in orphan drugs.

Getting Back on the Bicycle—Second Case Study

A medical device development company had developed a novel device for a difficult-to-treat condition. Attempts to find a strategic partner to commercialize the product resulted in only two low-ball offers—neither of which would have provided a return to the private investors who had funded the company since its inception. Effectively, no one showed up for the auction. A lack of statistically significant clinical data was felt to be the reason for the poor response.

Before deciding to accept one of the low-ball offers, the company reviewed the limited available clinical data. They were surprised to find that their device was effective in treating patients who had failed standard therapy. A device that would successfully treat these patients would be worth a great deal more than the offers on the table. The company decided that the benefits of a successful trial with patients who had failed previous therapy was worth the cost and risk. The trial is on-going.

What If There is Only One Potential Buyer?

Occasionally, there is only one potential buyer for a Small Company's technology. This situation arises when the one potential buyer has intellectual property that prevents others from using the Small Company's technology. Examples: a drug delivery technology that works only with a patent protected protein; a cranial device that depends on a one-of-a-kind catheter for delivery.

Holding an auction is impossible. The Large Company is well aware that its intellectual property position locks out others. Nevertheless, the Small Company's technology may have a very high value to its one potential buyer. The technology may improve the Large Company's competitive position (e.g., a drug delivery technology enabling a branded pharmaceutical product to compete with generics) or allow the Large Company to expand into new market segments (e.g., a coating enabling a wound closure device to be used instead of sutures).

Now, the Small Company's challenge is getting a transaction recognizing the value of its technology. Creating a well-informed potential buyer is as important when there is one potential buyer as when there are many potential buyers. By convincing the Large Company of the value of their technology, the Small Company has created a more level playing field. The Small Company's arguments in support of its technology must be especially compelling because the Large Company, as the only potential buyer, has every reason not to accept them. Once they accept that the Small Company's technology is a singular asset of high value to them, the Large Company has no motivation to risk not getting a transaction done. Both parties have strong reasons to conclude a transaction.

Of course, the Large Company can put a low-ball offer on the table no matter how convincing the Small Company is. The Small Company's appropriate response is a whole-pie analysis showing the size of each party's slice should the proposed terms be accepted. The whole pie analysis highlights how much value the Large Company would lose by failing to acquire the technology. The Small Company's success in communicating the value of its technology is essential to establishing the whole pie valuation.

The Small Company should be willing to walk away should the Large Company insist on unfair terms. Yet, another reason to avoid being under pressure to close a transaction.

CHAPTER 13

CHOOSING THE RIGHT LARGE COMPANY

The right Large Company can be critical to the successful development of the Small Company's technology and to the Small Company receiving milestone payments and royalties. Attracting several potential buyers, an auction gives the Small Company a choice of Large Companies. Financial terms dictate the choice in most cases. The choice may also depend on which potential bidder appears best suited to bring the technology to commercialization. The importance of choosing the right Large Company varies directly with the size of late milestone payments and the royalty rate. Enormous late milestone payments and double digit royalties look very attractive on a term sheet. Whether or not the Small Company sees any of this depends, at least to some extent, on its choice of Large Company.

Stewardship

Upon entering into a business development transaction, the Small Company turns over stewardship of its technology to the Large Company. Successful development of the Small Company's technology now depends on how well the technology performs in the hands of the Large Company, the competence of the Large Company in managing the project, and the Large Company's often arcane internal resource allocation issues (i.e., how much the Large Company spends on R&D, on which projects it spends its R&D dollars, and the quality of the resources it devotes to each project). All are outside the control of the Small Company. (Sending your only child to a four-year boarding school in a distant location with intermittent phone and email service is roughly analogous.)

Understandably, Small Companies have high anxiety about doing this. As we will discuss, choosing the right Large Company is the way to ameliorate the anxiety. Contractual terms, such as "Best Efforts" clauses, are valuable, but not nearly as effective.

Stewardship—Parable Part 1

Brett Canfield is an outstanding high school football player—starter all four years, All-County as a sophomore, All-State as a junior and senior. Mr. and Mrs. Canfield are convinced that their son has the potential to become an All-American, and then move to a brilliant, financially rewarding, career in the NFL. Recruiters from several major college football programs have contacted the Canfields; a football scholarship is a virtual certainty. The proud parents and son have decided together that they want a football program that will make every reasonable effort to turn Brett into an All-American, barring a major injury. This is their definition of stewardship.

The college recruiters agree that Brett certainly has the potential to become an All-American. The recruiters also know that their #1 objective is to build a winning football team. Recruiting promising athletes, such as Brett, and turning them into All-Americans is an objective only so far as it supports building a winning football program. The recruiters have other considerations: how will Brett's skills, strength, and maturity develop over the next four years; how will Brett compare to other All-State players, many with similar capabilities, competing for his position; what happens should there be a change in coaching philosophy so that Brett's particular abilities are less valuable. Recruiters from each school explain their objectives and concerns. The recruiters propose the following: "Our coaching staffs will put their best efforts toward developing your son according to his talent, work ethic, and fit with our program." This is the recruiters' definition of stewardship.

The Canfields are unhappy with the large gap between the respective definitions of stewardship. The definition of stewardship is not a point of negotiation. Using negotiating power, i.e., by taking advantage of the competition among recruiters, is useless. The Canfields, now understanding the recruiters' objectives, realize that a recruiter who accepts their definition of stewardship is agreeing to something that cannot be delivered. Honest recruiters cannot accept their definition. Knowing that Brett can only become an All-American by participating in a major college football program, they accept, grudgingly, the recruiters' definition of stewardship.

In the world of life-science business development transactions, Mr. and Mrs. Canfield represent the Small Company, Brett is the Small Company's technology, the college football program is the Large Company, and what the coaches define as stewardship describes "best efforts." Just as the college coaching staff, if they are honest, cannot assure the parents that they will do everything possible to turn their son into an All American, a Large Company, if it is honest, cannot assure the Small Company that developing the Small Company's technology will be its number one priority. Should the Small Company follow the Canfield's example or stick to its guns?

"Best Efforts" Clauses

Small Companies try to assure the Large Company performs its stewardship responsibilities by having a "Best Efforts" clause in the transaction contract. "Best Efforts" clauses describe the Large Company's stewardship responsibilities. Small Companies want "Best Efforts" clauses written to obligate the Large Company to do everything possible to make the technology a success. Large Companies want "Best Efforts" clauses written to preserve their flexibility and minimize their obligations.

The harder the Large Company pushes for a weak "Best Efforts" clause the more suspicious the Small Company becomes about the Large Company's intentions. The harder the Small Company pushes for a strong "Best Efforts" the more suspicious the Large Company becomes. The wording of the "Best Efforts" clause often becomes highly contentious, engendering a great deal of ill-will. More often than, not the final product is a murky compromise.

The following is a "Best Efforts" clause from an actual contract. Attorneys for both sides have told us it is one of the strongest "Best Efforts" clauses they have seen.

> "Best Commercial Efforts" shall mean those consistent and diligent efforts and resources that a leading pharmaceutical company, such as Large Company, would use in order to develop (including conducting preclinical and clinical trials), obtain Regulatory Approval(s) for, manufacture, promote, detail and market, as the case may be, a new pharmaceutical product with significant commercial potential taking into account commercial considerations, including without limitation issues of safety and efficacy, product profile, the proprietary position of the Licensed Product, the regulatory environment and status of the Licensed Product and other relevant scientific, technical, business, and economic factors."

Is this supposedly strong "Best Efforts" clause a guarantee that development of the Licensed Product will get priority over everything else? Or that the Large Company will not acquire similar technology from another source or develop similar technology on their own? Or not abandon the Licensed Product under almost any circumstances? Of course not. All that this "Best Efforts" clause says is that the Large Company will take a reasoned, business-like approach to developing the Licensed Product.

There are other limitations. "Best Efforts" can vary widely among Large Companies. For example, "Best Efforts" of Large Company with strong distribution in the EU are going to be very different from "Best Efforts" of a Large Company with almost all of its sales generated in North America. Another example: "Best Efforts" of a Large Company with no internally developed alternatives to the Small Company's technology may be very different from the "Best Efforts" of a Large Company with an internally developed alternative.

The utility of "Best Efforts" clauses is further limited by the fact that over the term of a long relationship typical of life-science business development agreements, often a decade or more, things change, often in drastic and unexpected ways. Even the most prescient cannot foresee all the changes in the next ten, or even five, years in the regulatory, reimbursement, science, clinical, or competitive environment, or within the Large Company itself, which may affect the development of the technology. For example, the availability of effective vaccines for ovarian cancer will reduce the market potential for a small molecule drug therapy for the treatment of ovarian cancer. The Large Company developing the small molecule drug may very well conclude that the investment required to bring the drug to market no longer justifies best efforts as was intended in the transaction signed several years earlier.

The Limits of a "Best Efforts" Clause—Case Study

The project for which we negotiated the above "best efforts" clause was moving along according to schedule. That is, until our client's strategic partner was acquired by an even larger Large Company. Our client's new strategic partner is, of course, obligated to the terms of the original contract, including the "best efforts" clause. Their interpretation of the meaning of "best efforts," however, appears to differ from that of the original partner. The new strategic partner has fired all of the scientists who had been working on the project prior to the acquisition.

"Best Efforts" clauses provide limited assurance to Small Companies. Lengthy negotiations on a "Best Efforts" clause are seldom worth the time, cost, and acrimony. The best assurances the Small Company can get is to choose the right Large Company. And as highlighted by the above case study, even choosing the right Large Company does not provide total protection.

Choosing the Right Large Company

The Canfields and the Small Company find themselves in the same boat. To get their respective projects underway, they have to accept definitions of stewardship that fall far short of what they wanted at the beginning. Both need to find a better way to assuage their sense of anxiety.

Stewardship—Parable Part 2

The Canfields' grudging acceptance of the recruiters' definitions of stewardship does nothing to help them select the best football program for Brett. With little variation among recruiters' definitions, they have no criteria for making a selection.

Towards the end of football season, Coach Maucry asks Brett about his choice of a major college football program. Brett takes a deep breath and relates the sad story. Coach Maucry smiles, "Son, in my 25 years of coaching I have had the privilege of having only a handful of boys with your potential. I am disappointed to say not one of you learned anything from watching me week in and week out do everything I could to learn everything possible about next Saturday's opponents."

"What does scouting out the opposition have to do with choosing a college football program?" Brett replies reinforcing Coach Maucry's disappointment.

"I'll tell you what I told the other hot shots. At the beginning of each season, I know next to nothing about the teams on our schedule. Scouting is the only way I can get the information I need to decide how we're going to approach the upcoming game."

"What do you know about the college football programs you've been considering? Less than I know about the teams we'll face next year. You and your parents are frustrated because you can't get a guarantee. Nobody gets one. Go out and do some scouting. Find out how successful each program has been in developing young athletes, how many All-Americans they have produced, who from their school has gone on to a successful professional career, their development plan for you. When you find out everything you can then make a decision."

To evaluate how well a Large Company will exercise its stewardship responsibilities, the Small Company should examine the Large Company's track record and evaluate the Large Company's plans for its technology. Discussions with other Small Companies who have done transactions with the Large Company can help establish the Large Company's track record. Discussions should focus on:

- Frequency and quality of communications about project status
- Demonstrations of commitment to project success
- Resolution of problems
- Disengagement (if the project was not successful)
- Working relationships between personnel of the two companies
- Willingness to do another transaction with this company.

As part of its decision to turn over stewardship of its technology to a Large Company, the Small Company should know how the Large Company intends to develop the technology and commercialize a resulting product, should there be one. It is appropriate and legitimate for the Small Company to get answers to critical questions from the Large Company.

- How are you planning to develop the technology?
- Who will be responsible for the project?
- Why do you believe you can be successful?
- What clinical indications do you intend to pursue? Why these?
- How will you structure clinical trials to confirm these indications and position the product for reimbursement?
- What would cause you to decide the project should be terminated?
- What is your regulatory strategy for each major market, e.g. the U.S., the EU, Japan?
- What does your development schedule look like?
- How will you launch the product? With what resources? What are your expected sales?
- How will you deal with specific situations, such as the new product cannibalizing one of your existing products?

How a Large Company responds indicates whether or not it will be a good steward. A Large Company that responds in an open and straightforward manner will almost certainly be a better choice than the Large Company whose grudging response is circumspect or incomplete.

Small Companies should not be reticent to ask these questions. A Large Company asks many more questions than these to understand and evaluate the Small Company's technology. The Small Company has similar rights.

Benefits of Choosing the Right Partner

The choice of the right Large Company is especially important when the program hits some bumps in the road, a change in market conditions, or a change in the Large Company's strategy or key personnel. The right Large Company will, in these circumstances, more than likely attempt to work with the Small Company to resolve the problems and to find how the program may be altered to respond to changed circumstances. The following case study is an innovative approach to problem resolution worked out by the senior executives of a Small Company and a Large Company. What is summarized below was included in the contract. The president of the Small Company had convincing evidence that he had chosen the right Large Company.

Solving Problems Cooperatively—Case Study

The Small Company's CEO and the Large Company's senior executive in charge of the business segment acquiring the technology agreed to have quarterly meetings. The meeting agendas were set by these two individuals. The agenda items always included having the senior scientists from the Large Company report on project progress and goals for the next quarter. The Small Company's CEO, his senior scientists, and independent outside advisors were allowed to attend the meeting.

Scientists from both parties were encouraged by the two senior executives to work together to address technical problems identified at the meetings. The Large Company had final decision making responsibility on technical problem resolution.

Any serious disagreements over the level and quality of the Large Company's efforts would be discussed by the Small Company's CEO and Large Company's senior executive. Should these discussions fail to resolve the disagreements, the Small Company had the right to reclaim its technology and to negotiate for cash in compensation for the Large Company not applying its best effort.

These terms worked for both parties in several ways.

- Communication and issue resolution were regular, flexible, and targeted at resolving problems early on.
    - The Small Company's CEO and his management team were kept informed of project progress and were able, by setting the agenda, to focus on issues of importance to them.
    - Mechanisms for problem resolution were in place. The parties were expected to resolve problems. Terminating the transaction was a last resort.
- Each party had implicit reasons to avoid terminating the transaction.
    - The project was of strategic importance to the Large Company. The embarrassment of a public disclosure stating the Small Company was pulling out and the write-off of a rather large upfront payment provided additional motivation to resolve issues.
    - Once the Small Company announced its decision to terminate the transaction, the Large Company would stop working on the project. Transferring the technology would take several months; negotiating compensation another few months; finding another Large Company to take over the project, uncertain?

During a recent lunch, we asked the president of the Small Company how this project was doing. He smiled and told us that the most recent meeting had been a week ago. Everything was on schedule. His counterpart at the Large Company told him to expect the next milestone payment by the end of the year, several months earlier than had been anticipated.

CHAPTER 14

MANAGING BUSINESS DEVELOPMENT

Our focus has been on what we have found to be an effective business development process. We would be remiss, however, to end without commenting on four important issues affecting how business development is managed. These are: the best time to initiate a business development effort, providing adequate resources for business development, the role of the Small Company's CEO, and how to choose between hiring a V.P. of Business Development and engaging a professional transaction advisor.

The Best Time to Initiate a Business Development Effort

Initiating a business development effort occurs when the Small Company decides to aggressively seek acquirers or partners for its technology. Activities to create well-informed potential buyers, such as presenting at scientific and industry conferences should be on-going and should begin well before the transaction process is initiated. We advise clients to begin creating well-informed potential buyers as soon as there is adequate IP protection and there is sufficient data to begin making the case for the technology.

Clearly, the value of the technology increases with the quality and quantity of information about the technology (assuming, of course, that the information is generally positive). The quality and quantity of information increases value because there is less to be done going forward and some of the risks of failure have been eliminated. In addition, the availability of more quality information improves the ability of the Small Company to use the auction process to level the playing field. The chart below summarizes how a technology's stage of development, here used as a proxy for information quantity and quality, affects the power of an auction.

Technology Stage of Development and Key Elements of the Auction Process

Elements of the Auction Process	Stage of Development—Pre Proof of Concept	Stage of Development—Proof-of-Concept Demonstrated
Number of Potential Buyers	Few, if any, Large Companies willing to invest in unproven technology	Several
Valuation of the Technology	Difficult due to large number of uncertainties.	Less difficult, some uncertainties have been resolved, possible to estimate using industry norms
Ability of Small Company to Create Well-Informed Potential Buyers	Low—there is little information about the technology available	High—information about safety and efficacy and support for the technology as a singular asset

Thus, having more and higher quality information increases the value of the technology and makes it more likely that an auction will allow the Small Company to realize that value.

Increasing the quality and quantity of information about a technology requires resources. Some Small Companies may want to move their technology only so far. Other Small Companies developing more than one technology, or a technology with several therapeutic uses, may find themselves unable to pursue their technology's full potential.

The best time to initiate a business development effort is when the technology has demonstrated proof-of-concept. Where the Small Company lacks the resources to take its technology this far, the technology should be developed as far as possible in one disease target before beginning a business development initiative. Initiating a business development effort too early is, in our experience, one of the biggest factors in an auction either failing to attract any potential buyers or resulting in no potential buyer submitting satisfactory terms.

Providing Adequate Business Development Resources

The business development process described in this Guide requires a commitment of Small Company resources. R&D people have to be available to prepare and make presentations at scientific and industry conferences as well as to interact with their counter-parts at Large Companies interested in the technology. The Small Company's CEO certainly has to lead and be involved in the process (the CEO's role is the subject of the next section). When the CEO and R&D people lack business development expertise or the time to devote to business development, the Small Company needs to hire a V.P. Business Development or engage a professional transaction advisor.

Whether or not it makes sense to provide all the resources necessary for a business development effort depends on the potential for the resulting transaction to yield sufficient value to justify this allocation of resources. The factors affecting the likelihood of a business development effort yielding a satisfactory return are summarized in the table below.

Likelihood of a Satisfactory Return from
Fully Funded Business Development Effort

	High	Low
Objective of the Transaction	Realize substantial value from the technology	Raise money quickly or validate the technology
Technology's State of Development	At or close to proof-of-concept	Early stage or intellectual property only
Strategic importance to buyer	Very important	Unimportant or unknown
Size of Transaction	Large	Small

There is, of course, a large area of gray shading between the two extremes on the table. Careful evaluation is needed to decide where in the spectrum each specific opportunity sits and how its position affects the likelihood of having a satisfactory return on business development spending.

In summary, there is little reason to devote expensive resources to initiating a business development transaction that has a low likelihood of generating a satisfactory return. The Small Company could be better off waiting until a transaction has sufficient potential to justify devoting needed resources to business development. On the other hand, it is equally unwise to provide fewer resources than needed when a transaction has the potential to yield a satisfactory return.

The Role of the Small Company CEO

A business development transaction that has the potential to create significant value for the Small Company and its shareholders seems to us to be the responsibility of the Small Company's CEO. The involvement of the CEO in successful business development transactions is typically focused on:

- Creating reasonable expectations from his Board and investors for the transaction based on a careful assessment of the value of his company's technology
- Assuring that the scientists, clinicians and engineers, who have other priorities, play an active part in attracting potential buyers and creating well-informed buyers
- Networking to attract potential buyers
- Assuring adequate business development resources
- Keeping the auction going as long as possible by keeping the board of directors informed as to the progress of the business development process
- Guiding negotiations, especially where the parties cannot seem to come to an agreement on key terms.

How a CEO can guide negotiations to a successful conclusion is illustrated in the following case study.

Closing The Gap

Almadian Pharma was engaged in a long, difficult negotiation with a Large Company. Every term had been argued, discussed, and re-argued before the two sides came to agreement. Most of the major issues were resolved, except for the amount of the upfront payment. Almadian's CEO, Tobias Trently, had at the start of the negotiations insisted on an upfront payment of at least $75 million. Almadian's negotiating team had stuck to this target. The Large Company's team was equally adamant about an upfront payment no larger than $65 million. Negotiations were stalled, and two successive negotiating sessions were cancelled.

Trently called a meeting with his negotiating team. Convinced that the Large Company was unlikely to change its position, Trently asked his negotiating team whether the Large Company would add a $10 million payment, based on achieving a near-term milestone, if Almadian agreed to the $65 million upfront payment. The negotiating team thought it was possible and argued that the $10 million payment should be $12 million to account for the time value of money. Trently told his team, "We've got a great deal with a great company. Let's not screw this up for $2 million."

As CEO, Trently was the only person in the company to make the decision to reduce the upfront payment and accept the reduction in the form of a near-term milestone payment.

Trently met the executive from the Large Company responsible for the transaction at a very expensive restaurant. Over dinner, he told the executive that he wanted to do the transaction with the Large Company but would only do so with an upfront payment of $65 million and a $10 million near-term milestone. Trently also told the executive that this was the last item to be negotiated. Trently, as CEO, was the only person who could make this definitive statement.

The final transaction had a $65 million upfront payment and Almadian received the $10 million milestone payment ten months after the transaction closed.

Many Small Company CEOs want to participate in all of the face-to-face negotiations. We advise against this, even when the CEO has excellent negotiating skills. One reason is that the senior decision maker from the Large Company is usually not involved in the face-to-face negotiations. With their decision maker not in the room, the Large Company negotiators will ask to consult with their senior decision maker before committing to any major term in the contract. By being present, the Small Company CEO may feel forced to make decisions immediately. During negotiations between Large and Small Companies, the following is not atypical (if, somewhat overly dramatic).

> Large Company: "We could agree to a larger upfront payment of $X if you can agree to drop a near-term milestone payment and reduce the milestone payment at regulatory approval by $Y.

> Small Company (with CEO present): "That sounds reasonable to us."

> Large Company: "O.K. We'll confirm with our EVP."

> Later,
> Large Company: "Our EVP and CFO have told us, we cannot make an upfront payment of more than $Z due to accounting issues. ($Z is considerably less than $X) Would that be acceptable?

The Small Company with their CEO present made a definitive decision regarding the terms offered by the Large Company. Whereas, the Large Company took time to discuss its next steps with the additional advantage of knowing how much the Small Company was willing to give. The Small Company's negotiating team would have been better off had their CEO not been there and they, too, would have had to check with headquarters before committing.

Our second reason for advising against the CEO being involved in face-to-face negotiations is that following most business development transactions there will be an on-going relationship between the two parties. Heated arguments during negotiations can harm, and often poison, this relationship. Being absent, the Small Company CEO avoids being part of this and can step in as the senior statesman to calm the troubled waters.

Does the Business Development Process Require a Vice President of Business Development?

Though the CEO has responsibility for the business development process, the CEO should not do all, or in our view, even most, of the work. Casting a net widely to attract potential buyers, preparing and distributing presentation materials, valuing the technology, and negotiating transaction terms are all very time consuming. The CEO's time and effort are better spent elsewhere. On the other hand, executing the business development process should not be neglected or delegated entirely to an administrative assistant. As we have suggested, the results of a transaction depend on how well the business development process is executed. Good execution, in turn, depends on involving a knowledgeable senior business development professional.

Engaging a senior business development professional can be worthwhile even when a technology does not warrant a fully resourced business development effort, in-house business development has solicited term sheets, or a Large Company submits an unexpected bid. Here, the senior business development professional brings negotiating skills and Large Company transaction experience that may be in short supply at the Small Company. Her skills and experience can provide appropriate responses to term sheets and can help negotiate the best possible business and financial terms. In addition, the business development professional can help the Small Company avoid costly mistakes in critical transaction business terms.

To meet their need for a senior business development person, some Small Companies hire a V.P. of Business Development. Others engage transaction advisors such as our firm, HVA, Inc. Strong arguments can be made for each alternative. We will outline both sides of the argument as fairly as possible and leave the decision to the Small Company CEO.

Arguments in Support of Hiring a V.P. of Business Development:

- The V.P. Business Development becomes part of the senior management team and can contribute more broadly than the business development process.
- The V.P. Business Development builds a deep understanding of the Small Company's technology, which becomes especially important when there are several business development transactions to be done.
- The V.P. Business Development has a vested interest in the long-term success of the Small Company.

Arguments in Support of Hiring a Transaction Advisory Firm:

- Jointly, the principals of a transaction advisory firm have broader industry knowledge, a wider network of contacts, more transaction experience, and better negotiating skills than most Senior Business Development executives.
- The transaction advisory firm is highly motivated to do the best possible deal as the biggest part of their compensation, the success fee, is typically tied to the financial terms of the transaction.
- Once the engagement is completed, the Small Company has no on-going fixed expenses.

The Small Company can benefit from having a V.P. of Business Development and engaging a transaction advisor. Having both can be particularly valuable when a transaction is substantial or the Large Company has a reputation as a difficult negotiator. Here, the advisor should be engaged just prior to submission of term sheets from Large Companies. A transaction advisor can also add value when the advisor has significantly more knowledge about an industry segment than does the V.P. A medical device company seeking to do a transaction with a pharmaceutical company would be well advised to engage an advisor familiar with how pharmaceutical companies work.

Whichever the choice, the V.P. of Business Development or the transaction advisors should have the knowledge about how Large Companies make technology acquisition decisions. The business development effort always has the objective of "selling" the Small Company's technology to a Large Company. Knowing the customer is as important in life-science business development as in any other type of sales transaction.

The Small Company should have access to business development expertise focused on realizing as much value from each transaction as possible. This is very different from having a track record of closing many transactions. Closing many transactions is easy. Closing transactions that realize significant value takes much more effort. Having access to expertise that knows how to close transactions that realize value is worth much, much more than having access to expertise in closing transactions.

CONCLUSION

At its heart, *Leveling the Playing Field* is about the value of innovative life-science technology. Value attracts Large Companies, value creates the opportunity for an "auction," and value induces the buyer to compensate appropriately to acquire the technology. For Large Companies, value comes from their perception that the technology can lead them to a strategically important product faster, less expensively, or at lower risk than their alternatives.

A technology's value, or more accurately, perceived value, reflects a large number of assumptions about the time and cost for the technology to yield a commercially successful product and the risk of it failing to do so. Alternatives to the technology, or the strategic importance of the product resulting from the technology, also affect its perceived value. Not surprisingly, perceptions about a technology's value vary widely among potential buyers. Our "auction" model makes it more likely that the Large Company putting the highest valuation on the technology will be the eventual buyer at the highest possible price.

Successful business development comes from a well-executed business development process working with a well-developed technology. This Guide describes what we have found to be an effective business development process. The Guide's approach to business development, or any other approach, works only when there is real value in the Small Company's technology. Returning to our art auction analogy, a major art auction house, with all its experience and skill, can do little with a painting of little value.

The Small Company wanting to generate the best possible return for its investors and employees should be focused on the one objective of creating value from its technologies. Every Small Company believes this is what they are doing. Using the principles of the Guide, we suggest the following as measures of how well the Small Company is creating value.

- Identification of an important indication where their technology can be shown to be a singular asset
- Producing data to support claims of their technology being a singular asset
- Careful selection of projects so there are resources to bring those selected to demonstration of proof-of-principle or beyond
- Making presentations and publications to their scientific and clinical communities
- Creating strong intellectual property protection and obtaining a freedom to operate opinion.

We have, quite deliberately, said little about what constitutes value to the Small Company. Financial terms of the transaction—upfront payment, milestone payments, royalties—certainly are the major constituents of value. The ability to choose a Large Company with a strong commitment to and capability of developing the technology can become a major determinant of value. This is especially important where late stage milestone payments and royalties make up the substantial part of the Small Company's financial returns.

The ability to structure the transaction to be tax advantageous to the Small Company and its shareholders, the Small Company providing on-going post-transaction development support, and the Small Company's rights to continue using its technology in other therapeutic areas and geographies can provide additional value. How value is received depends on issues and factors specific to each Small Company and each transaction. There are no general rules or guidelines. What we can suggest is that the Small Company decides what it values and then use their business development process to get the highest possible value.

Development of innovative life-science technologies is a difficult business. Failure is much more common than success. "Leveling the Playing Field" was written so that the successful developer of an innovative life-science technology can, indeed, recognize the value created.

BIBLIOGRAPHY

Auction Theory

Ausubel, Lawrence M., Milgrom, Paul, "The Lovely but Lonely Vickrey Auction" Combinatorial Auctions, pp 17–40, 2006, MIT Press

Becker, Thomas C., "Theory and Practice of Auctions" February 2001, Proceedings of the 75th Seminar of the European Association of Agricultural Economists

Board, Simon, "Economics 2102: Auctions, Bargaining and Pricing," Fall 2004, University of Toronto

Isaace Mark, Salmon, Timothy, Zillante, Arthur, "A Theory of Jump Bidding in Ascending Auctions," January 2004, Department of Economics, Florida State University

Keenes, John, "Competitive Auctions: Theory and Applications," September 2004, Centre for Applied Microeconometrics, Institute of Economics, University of Copenhagen

Krishna, Vijay, *Auction Theory* 2002, Academic Press, San Diego, CA

Milgrom, Paul *Putting Auction Theory to Work,* 2005, Cambridge University Press, Cambridge, UK

Milgrom, Paul, Weber Robert J, "A Theory of Auctions and Competitive Bidding," September 1982, Econometrica

Milgrom, Paul, Weber, Robert J. "The Value of Information in a Sealed-Bid Auction," 1982, North Holland

Nikutta, Jörg, "Three Essays in the Theory of Auctions" February 2003, Doctoral Dissertation, University of Mannheim

Warsh, David, "When Auction Theory Was Put to Work," May 21, 2006, economicprincipals.com

Zaretsky, Adam M., "Going once, going twice, sold: Auctions and the success of economic theory," January 1998, Federal Reserve Bank of St. Louis

Negotiating

Camp, Jim, *Starting With No*, 2002, Crown Business, New York

Cohen, Herb, *You Can Negotiate Anything,* 1980, Bantam Books, New York

Fisher, Roger and William Ury, *Getting to Yes*, 1991, Penguin Books, New York

Gotbaum, Victor, *Negotiating in the Real World*, 1999, Simon & Schuster, New York

Ury, William, *Getting Past No*, 1993, Bantam Books, New York

NONCONFIDENTIAL
EXECUTIVE SUMMARIES

Following are three NonConfidential Executive Summaries we produced for clients. The three technologies were still in development at the time the Executive Summaries were written. Consequently, the Executive Summaries emphasize technical, clinical, and regulatory issues. These Executive Summaries are intended to illustrate many of the conclusions and recommendations in this <u>Guide</u>. They are not, in anyway whatsoever, a solicitation to enter into a transaction with the sponsoring company.

Each Executive Summary addresses a different market and competitive situation.

- HYDROBOOT is a medical device technology targeted at a market that has seen little innovation in the last 25 years. Existing products were, for the most part, seen as commodities and receive little if any promotional support. Medicare reimbursement in the U.S. and E.U. is minimal.
- CHRONOCORT™ is expected to be an improved pharmaceutical treatment for patients with Adrenal Insufficiency (AI) and Chronic Adrenal Hyperplasia (CAH). CHRONOCORT™ is a specialty pharmaceutical as AI and CAH are treated by endocrinologists. Currently low cost, partially effective generic drugs are used to treat these diseases. The patient population in the U.S. and the E.U. is 250,000.

- SATIVEX® is a derivative of cannabis with demonstrated capabilities to treat severe pain which no longer responds to opioid treatment. To be commercialized in the U.S, SATIVEX® had to demonstrate efficacy in Phase III clinical trials and get DEA approval to distribute.

INCAPPE® INC.

HYDROBOOT

CREATING GROWTH OPPORTUNITIES IN WOUND CARE

EXCLUSIVE PARTNERSHIP OPPORTUNITY

Prepared by HVA, Inc.
Advisory Services for Life-Science Transactions
October 10, 2006

LARGE, NEW WOUNDCARE MARKET SEGMENT

Opportunities to create new wound care market segments are rare. HYDROBOOT, a new compression therapy device, is such an opportunity.

HYDROBOOT's new market segment includes patients with venous stasis ulcers and patients with severe chronic edema who have not responded to compression wrap therapy. HYDROBOOT has demonstrated effectiveness with both groups of these difficult-to-treat patients.

In addition to its use for patients who have not responded to compression wrap therapy, HYDROBOOT's market segment may include other indications where compression wraps are contra-indicated or have minimal effectiveness. These indications include: venous stasis ulcer patients with concomitant arterial disease, venous stasis ulcer patients who may benefit from daily application of local therapies, and for athletes and others with acute trauma induced swelling. HYDROBOOT has no, or very limited, competition from compression wraps for these indications.

Sales potential for indications where HYDROBOOT has little or no competition from compression wraps is estimated to be $150–$250 million globally. This market estimate does not include HYDROBOOT's use with patients who find compression wraps too uncomfortable to wear. These patients could increase HYDROBOOT's market to as much as $200–$300 million.

HYDROBOOT's lead application is in venous stasis ulcer patients and patients with severe edema who have not responded to compression wraps. Whether these patients discontinue compression therapy entirely or convert to pneumatic compression therapy, they are no longer part of the compression wrap market segment. By providing a new treatment option for these patients, HYDROBOOT creates a large, new segment of the compression therapy market. HYDROBOOT has no competition from compression wraps in this segment.

The number of patients in this new market segment is substantial. As many as half of the 2 million patients worldwide now being treated for venous stasis ulcers do not respond to standard compression wrap therapy[2]. An additional 2 million patients are believed to be receiving no treatment at all—many because of prior unsatisfactory experiences with compression wraps. 14 million patients in the United States with venous insufficiency have the potential to develop severe edema.

---

2   U.S. Compression Therapy Wound Care Market, Frost & Sullivan 2000.

HYDROBOOT has FDA 510(k) clearance. HYDROBOOT is covered by an issued U.S. patent; action by the EU patent office is pending.

INCAPPE®, a private medical device company which has developed HYDROBOOT, is seeking an exclusive strategic partner committed to pursuing this opportunity.

HYDROBOOT—DIFFERENT IN CONCEPT AND DESIGN

HYDROBOOT is different in design and concept from compression wraps and from pneumatic compression therapy devices. HYDROBOOT's design incorporates the best features of both and avoids their problems.

Specifically,

- HYDROBOOT consistently delivers optimum compression pressures from the ankle to the knee.
- HYDROBOOT complements the natural action of the calf muscles in removing fluid from the lower leg by delivering a leg massaging pressure wave as the patient walks.
- HYDROBOOT patients are mobile. Patients can drive their car and walk while wearing the device.
- Patients wear HYDROBOOT throughout the day thereby getting 12 hours of benefit from the compression pressure wave. Patients using pneumatic compression therapy devices receive one to two hours of therapy per day.
- No special skill is required to put on HYDROBOOT. HYDROBOOT can be removed for bathing or sleeping and put back on by the patient or by the home care giver.
- HYDROBOOT is easily adjustable to accommodate day-to-day reduction in leg size as edema is reduced.
- Each HYDROBOOT can be worn for up to nine months. It withstands heavy use and is easy to clean.

HYDROBOOT COMPRESSION

HYDROBOOT's design uses the laws of fluid dynamics to deliver optimum compression pressure from the ankle to the knee. When the patient stands, the pull of gravity on the water contained in HYDROBOOT's inner bladder creates a pressure gradient. The pressure at any point along the length of the boot is determined by the height of the water column above that point. The height of the water column is greatest at the ankle and least just below the knee (at the top of HYDROBOOT's bladder). Thus, the compression pressure is highest at the ankle and declines in a consistent manner along the length of the device. By using the laws of fluid dynamics, HYDROBOOT delivers compression pressure equal to what wound care clinicians consider to be best practice when treating patients with compression wraps.

HYDROBOOT COMPRESSION—STANDING PATIENT

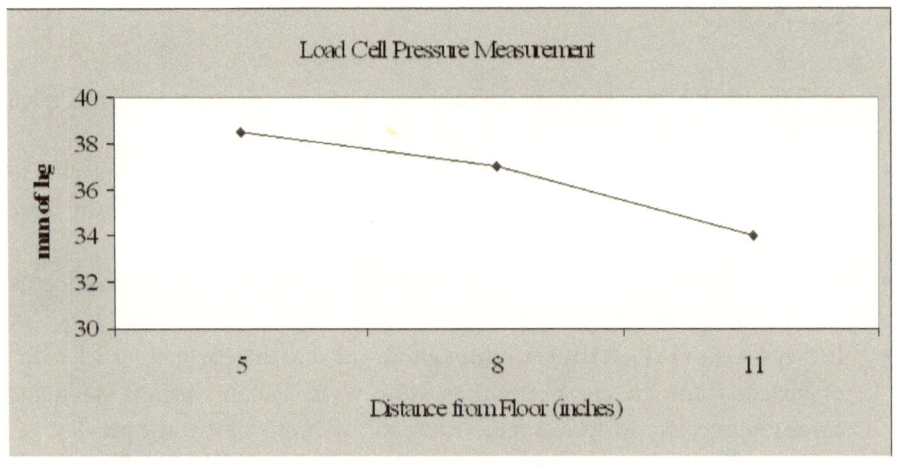

As the patient walks, HYDROBOOT's internal water-filled bladder delivers a pleasant leg-massaging compression wave, similar to that delivered by pneumatic compression therapy. Medicare and other payers reimburse for pneumatic compression therapy after a patient has not responded to at least six months of compression wrap therapy.

INCAPPE® believes that HYDROBOOT may provide superior outcomes when compared to pneumatic compression therapy. HYDROBOOT patients are ambulatory so that HYDROBOOT's compression wave works with the patient's circulatory system and action of the calf muscles to pump blood and fluid away from the lower extremities. Patients can and do wear HYDROBOOT throughout the day getting the benefits of compression waves for as much as 10—12 hours. In comparison, patients receive pneumatic pressure therapy for no more than two hours per day.

HYDROBOOT COMPRESSION WAVE—WALKING PATIENT

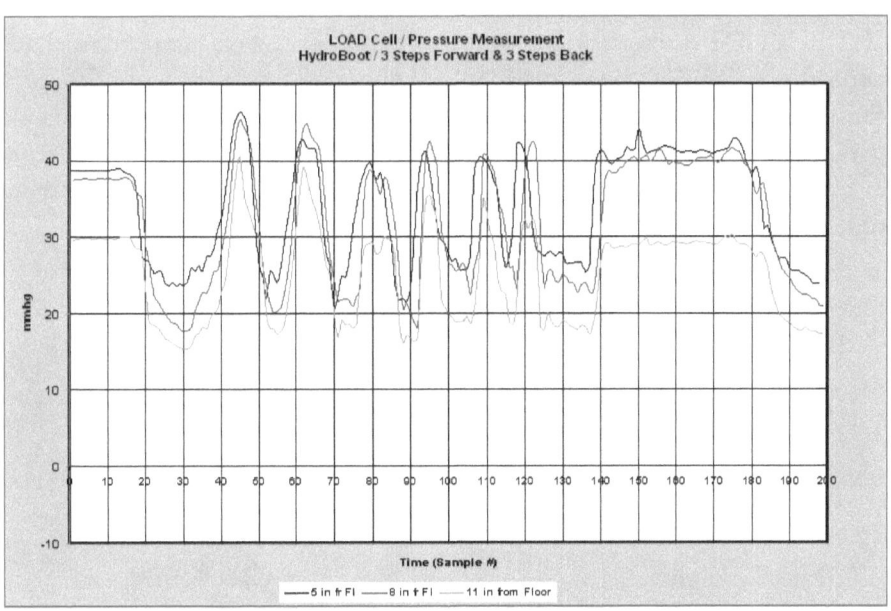

Putting on HYDROBOOT does not require extensive training or special techniques. Nurses at wound care clinics can teach most patients to put on HYDROBOOT in less than 30 minutes. The empty HYDROBOOT is put on, secured with three Velcro straps, and filled with tap water. Patients in the proof-of-principle clinical study were able to remove the HYDROBOOT to sleep comfortably and in the morning were able to reapply HYDROBOOT and refill the bladder achieving proper compression pressure. Patients were able to remove HYDROBOOT to bathe and to clean and redress the wound. The ability to remove and reapply makes HYDROBOOT an alternative to patients who find compression wraps too uncomfortable to wear continuously.

HYDROBOOT's Velcro straps allow HYDROBOOT to be easily readjusted to accommodate daily changes in leg size as edema is reduced. Compression wraps lose their effectiveness and become uncomfortable as edema is reduced between visits to the wound care clinic.

VENOUS STASIS ULCERS—PROOF-OF-CONCEPT CLINICAL TRIAL

HYDROBOOT demonstrated its ability to treat venous stasis ulcers that had not responded to Smith & Nephew's PROFORE® in a 15 patient proof-of-concept clinical trial. 10 patients were assigned to the HYDROBOOT arm and 5 patients to the PROFORE® arm. At Week 4, one patient discontinued PROFORE® due to discomfort and crossed over to HYDROBOOT. In all, eleven patients were treated with HYDROBOOT.

Ulcers completed healed for three HYDROBOOT patients. All three had previously been treated unsuccessfully with PROFORE®. Two patients, including the patient originally in the PROFORE® arm, achieved partial healing.

HYDROBOOT CLINICAL TRIAL OUTCOMES

Outcome	# of Patients
Healed	3—all previously failed PROFORE® therapy
Partially Healed	2—includes patient from PROFORE® arm (a)
Not Healed	1
Discontinued	5—none due to HYDROBOOT (b)
Total	11

The proof-of-concept clinical study was conducted by an independent wound-care clinic. Neither the clinic itself nor any member of the clinic's staff has a financial interest in INCAPPE® or HYDROBOOT.

Notes:

(a) The ulcers of the cross over patient decreased from 0.8 cm² to 0.15 cm² after 8 weeks of HYDROBOOT treatment. Had this patient completed the full 12 weeks of therapy, his ulcers may have healed completely.

(b) All five patients discontinued due to factors unrelated to HYDROBOOT.

The proof-of-concept clinical trial demonstrated that HYDROBOOT was more comfortable and patient friendly than PROFORE®. Two of the five PROFORE® patients discontinued due to discomfort. One of these patients went on to wear HYDROBOOT successfully until the conclusion of the twelve week study. No HYDROBOOT patient discontinued treatment due to discomfort.

Patients in the HYDROBOOT arm of the clinical trial were overwhelmingly positive in their evaluation of HYDROBOOT's comfort and ease of use.

HYDROBOOT CLINICAL TRIAL OUTCOMES
Patient Responses

Activity	# of Favorable Responses (9 total responses)
Putting on HYDROBOOT	8
Re-filling HYDROBOOT	7
Ease of Walking	8

SEVERE CHRONIC EDEMA

Many patients with severe chronic edema decide to discontinue therapy and live with their condition. These patients have increased risk of hospitalization due to sepsis and cellulites. Other chronic edema patients are converted to dynamic compression therapy. Short term studies by Henk Kuiper MD, HYDROBOOT's inventor, show HYDROBOOT to be effective for treating severe chronic edema even for difficult to treat patients.

Patient	Condition	Day 1	Outcome
119	400 lb male/chronic edema	Ankle: 21 ¼" Midcalf: 18" Knee: 22 ¼"	@ 2 weeks Ankle: 19 ¼" Midcalf: 17" Knee: 21 12"
131	Patient with leg ulcer since August of 2002	Calf: 22 ½"	@ 3 weeks Calf: 19 ¾" Wound size reduced
132	Diabetic patient suffering from severe edema of left leg. Previous right leg amputation	Calf: 20"	@ 2 weeks Calf: 18 ¾"; Boot no longer required
133	Patient with right leg wound for past 5 years	Calf: 20 ¼"	@ 1 week Calf: 15 ¾" Wound size reduced
136	2 year history of venous stasis ulcers	Calf: 17 ¼"	@ 2 ½ weeks Calf: 16 ¾" Wound 80% healed with granulation
137	5 year history of recurrent ulcers. HYDROBOOT applied one day following skin graft	Calf: 16"	@ 2 ½ weeks Calf: 14 ½" Significant wound healing

HYDROBOOT can reduce healthcare costs by reducing the risk of hospitalization for patients who discontinue therapy and by being a less expensive alternative than pneumatic compression therapy.

OTHER CLINICAL INDICATIONS

HYDROBOOT's revenue potential goes beyond venous stasis ulcers and severe chronic edema. Other indications include: patients with concomitant arterial disease, patients who may benefit from frequent applications of topical therapies, and acute swelling resulting from trauma.

Patients with Concomitant Arterial Disease

Patients with venous insufficiency and arterial disease need compression therapy for their venous insufficiency and periodically to have minimal compression pressure. Pressure from compression wraps can be reduced significantly only be removing the wrap. Consequently, compression wraps are contra-indicated for the approximately 20% of venous stasis ulcer patients with a brachial medial index of less than 0.8.

HYDROBOOT may be able to be used on these patients. Because HYDROBOOT's compression comes from gravity's pull on the water in HYDROBOOT's inner bladder, there is no pressure when the patient's leg is elevated. A venous stasis ulcer patient with concomitant arterial disease can relieve compression pressure by sitting down and putting his feet up.

More Frequent Applications of Topical Therapies

Patients or their at home care giver can apply topical therapy when they remove HYDROBOOT for bathing or sleeping. More frequent applications of local therapies may promote better wound healing outcomes.

Acute Swelling Following Trauma

Acute swelling following trauma is common in contact sports, especially football. Acute swelling from strains, sprains, post fractured ankle and similar injury can keep an athlete from playing or training for a prolonged period of time. Incappe® believes that HYDROBOOT can be as effective in treating acute swelling in otherwise healthy patients as it is in treating chronic edema in unhealthy patients. HYDROBOOT may allow the athlete to train while the injury heals.

Acute swelling has several important differences from other HYDROBOOT indications. The team, high school, college, or professional, and the athlete are motivated to have the injury heal as quickly as possible. The cost of a device which can accelerate the athlete's return to training or to play is often not an issue, especially at the college and professional level.

Clinical trials may be needed to confirm the utility of HYDROBOOT in these applications.

PRODUCT STATUS

HYDROBOOT has FDA 510(k) clearance and is covered by U.S. Patent 6945944 issued September 20, 2005. European Patent Application 03 18 081.7 is pending.

Incappe®, the company developing HYDROBOOT, has sought input from wound care nurses on how HYDROBOOT could provide even better ease of use and patient comfort. Their responses included: additional sizes to accommodate shorter patients and patients with very large calf sizes, and easier to use connections. Incappe® believes a limited amount of engineering would accommodate these changes and improve HYDROBOOT's manufacturability.

HYDROBOOT: A REVENUE GROWTH OPPORTUNITY

Standing alone in a new, large segment, HYDROBOOT is the first significant new revenue growth opportunity in compression therapy since the introduction of long-stretch multi-layer compression wraps. Incappe® is seeking an exclusive strategic partner to complete development of HYDROBOOT, secure reimbursement and aggressively pursue HYDROBOOT's $150–$200 million global revenue potential.

PHOQUS PHARMACEUTICALS LTD.

CHRONOCORT™

IMPROVED OUTCOMES FOR PATIENTS

with

CONGENITAL ADRENAL HYPERPLASIA

or

ADRENAL INSUFFICIENCY

STRATEGIC PARTNERSHIP OPPORTUNITY

Non-confidential Executive Summary
February 2007
Prepared by HVA, Inc. and BML, Ltd.
February 2007

INTRODUCTION

CHRONOCORT™ is being developed to improve outcomes for patients with adrenal insufficiency (AI) and congenital adrenal hyperplasia (CAH). Patients with AI and CAH are very sick, requiring replacement steroid therapy for the remainder of their lives. Current immediate release (IR) therapies—IR hydrocortisone, IR prednisone and IR dexamethasone—either have limited effectiveness or severe adverse side effects. Endorsements from key opinion leaders and patient support groups, and the granting of orphan drug status in the EU all support the need for more effective treatment for these very sick patients. With successful clinical development and the receipt of regulatory approval, CHRONOCORT™ could fulfill the widely recognized, currently unmet, need for more effective treatment and better outcomes.

IR drugs are limited by their inability to match a healthy adrenal gland's circadian rhythm production of cortisol. Patients typically have either too much or too little of the steroid replacements throughout the day. Short-and long-term adverse side effects from the current products are believed to result from this continuous mismatching.

CHRONOCORT™, using Phoqus' patented drug delivery technology, delivers hydrocortisone so as to mimic the cortisol release of a healthy adrenal gland.

CHRONOCORT™'s potential to improve significantly patient outcomes is matched by its commercial potential. The benefits of CHRONOCORT™ for the estimated 200,000 patients in the EU and US could result in very rapid market penetration at a significant price multiple versus current therapies. Peak year sales may exceed $200 million.

Further as AI and CAH are treated by endocrinologists, selling CHRONOCORT™ requires a relatively small sales force.

Phoqus, a publicly traded UK based company is seeking a strategic partner to complete the development and commercialize CHRONOCORT™. Becoming Phoqus' exclusive strategic partner has the following financial and strategic benefits.

- CHRONOCORT™, improving outcomes for patients poorly served by current therapies, has peak year sales potential in excess of $200 million.

- CHRONOCORT™ would be the first new treatment for AI and CAH in the past 40 years.

- AI and CAH are chronic conditions; patients take cortisol replacements for their entire lives.

- CHRONOCORT™ has been granted orphan drug status in the EU for CAH and has received a positive opinion for AI from the EMEA's Committee for Orphan Medical Products. The parallel status for Orphan Drug Indication has been filed in the U.S.

- Orphan drug status allows for smaller clinical trials, shortened time to market, and marketing exclusivity of seven (U.S.) or ten years (Europe).

- Low regulatory risk—CHRONOCORT™ has completed proof of principal trials in which it replicated the natural cortisol release cycle; CHRONOCORT™ is not an NCE.

- CHRONOCORT™ is protected by a robust patent portfolio.

The potential for CHRONOCORT™ rests on three factors:

(1) The identified need for a significantly better treatment for AI and CAH,

(2) CHRONOCORT™'s ability to penetrate the market rapidly with a premium price,

(3) CHRONOCORT™'s path to regulatory approval.

These will be addressed in the following sections.

THE IDENTIFIED NEED FOR AN IMPROVED TREATMENT

With an inadequate supply of cortisol, patients with AI and CAH are very ill. Left untreated, AI can result in death or a sharply reduced quality of life comparable to patients suffering from congestive heart failure. Untreated CAH can cause death, short stature, infertility, and adrenal and testicular tumors. Patients treated with currently approved steroid drugs do somewhat better but still suffer from a range of adverse side effects. Articles from peer reviewed journals describing the unsatisfactory outcomes of current treatments are available upon request.

The absence of satisfactorily effective treatments for AI and CAH has been recognized by the EMEA in granting orphan drug approval for CHRONOCORT™ in CAH and receiving favorable opinion from EMEA's Committee for Orphan Medical Products for CHRONOCORT™ in AI. EMEA guidelines require that for orphan drug designation a satisfactory method of treatment must not already exist. Phoqus expects FDA to agree with the EMEA's conclusion of a need for a much more effective treatment.

Additionally, CHRONCORT™ has the support of an advisory board consisting of leading endocrinologists, physicians at the National Institutes of Health, and patient advocacy groups including the CARES Foundation (www. caresfoundation.org).

MARKET PENETRATION AT A PREMIUM PRICE

Given the identified need for a safe and effective treatment very rapid market penetration should be expected for a product that improves outcomes for CAH and AI patients. An independent survey of prescribing physicians indicated almost 90% would consider CHRONOCORT™ as a first line treatment subject to its receiving regulatory approval.

Phoqus believes that the benefits of CHRONOCORT™ will justify a significant premium price over existing therapies. The same independent survey cited above indicated that a price per patient/year of $1,100–$1,300 would be acceptable. Phoqus is undertaking its own pricing study to confirm this. There are numerous precedents where products demonstrating significantly better outcomes sell at large premiums over branded or generic competition.

An annual selling price of $1,200 yields peak year sales in excess of $200 million as shown in CHRONOCORT™ COMMERCIAL POTENTIAL below.

CHRONOCORT™'s PATH TO REGULATORY APPROVAL

Market penetration and premium pricing depend on CHRONOCORT™ demonstrating superiority in pivotal clinical trials. Phoqus regulatory plans are based on a U.S. 505(b)(2) and an EU Abridged route. These routes provide the fastest time to filing while allowing claims of superiority to be demonstrated, and the potential for post-marketing studies. A US government funded body, recognized for its expertise in treating AI and CAH, is working closely with Phoqus to finalize the clinical trial protocol.

CHRONOCORT™ is projected to have regulatory approval by 2009.

The clinical trials will measure CHRONOCORT™'s effectiveness versus IR products in terms of improved PK reproducibility, reduced dosing, reduction in androgenic precursor 17-OHP in CAH patients, and improved quality of life for AI patients. The satisfactory control of 17-OHP correlates with the control of the disease in CAH. Details of Phoqus' clinical plans are available under a confidentiality agreement.

CHRONOCORT™ has a high likelihood of demonstrating these benefits. A clinical study demonstrated that hydrocortisone delivered by infusion to match the production of cortisol by a healthy adrenal gland provides the desired control of 17-OHP. Human clinical trials have shown that CHRONOCORT™, by employing Phoqus' unique, patented drug delivery technology can delivery hydrocortisone so as to match closely the release of cortisol by the healthy adrenal gland.

CHRONOCORT™ MARKET POTENTIAL

Peak year sales are estimated to be $200 million. The estimate assumes that CHRONOCORT™ performs successfully in clinical trials leading to approval and reimbursement at a significant premium over current products.

Current Patient Population of AI + CAH (2005)[1] (EU + US)	190,000
Expected Annual Growth Rate[2]	3%
Prevalence in 2012 (Three years following regulatory approval)	235,000
Anticipated Market Penetration[3]	75%
Number of Patients on CHRONOCORT™	175,300

Expected Annual Selling Price ($/patient/yr)[4] $1,200

CHRONOCORT™ Peak Year Sales $210 million

1   Population and prevalence studies
2   Increased rates of AI due to cancer therapies and autoimmune disease, (growth verified by IMS data)
3   Consistent with independent market research cited previously
4   Supported by independent market research; to be confirmed by Phoqus pricing study.

SUMMARY

CHRONOCORT™ can be a very attractive specialty pharmaceutical opportunity, especially for a company focused on chronic diseases. The recognized need for improved therapies for AI and CAH patients makes it likely that with successful clinical trials, CHRONOCORT™ will have rapid market penetration and secure reimbursement at a very significant premium to the IR drugs now used.

CHRONOCORT ™ has demonstrated in human clinical studies that it can mimic the circadian rhythm release of cortisol from a healthy adrenal gland. Studies in peer reviewed journals show that delivery of cortisol, via infusion, to match the body's circadian rhythm aligns the production of critically important 17-OHP with that of a healthy adrenal gland. Clinical studies will confirm that CHRONOCORT™ can produce the same results.

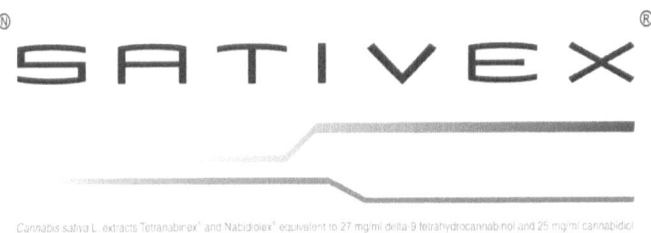

Cannabis sativa L. extracts Tetranabinex® and Nabidiolex® equivalent to 27 mg/ml delta 9 tetrahydrocannabinol and 25 mg/ml cannabidiol

- First-in-class drug with unique mechanism of action to treat severe pain.

Safety and efficacy in relieving cancer pain and neuropathic pain have been demonstrated successfully in nine European Phase III clinical trials.

- U.S. Phase III clinical trials for severe cancer pain begin in late 2006; NDA filing expected in 2008. Severe cancer pain is a $250–$500 million market.

- Follow-on indications are in the multi-billion dollar neuropathic pain market.

- Favorable responses from FDA and DEA minimize regulatory concerns.

- Differentiated pain product with franchise potential.

JULY, 2006

155

PARTNERING OPPORTUNITY FOR EXCLUSIVE US COMMERCIAL RIGHTS

SATIVEX®—a first-in-class drug with a unique mechanism of action to treat severe pain-will begin Phase III clinical trials for advanced cancer pain begin later this year. An NDA submission is scheduled for mid-2008. Approval to commercialize opens a $250–$500 million market opportunity in cancer pain. Additional Phase III clinical trials for other pain indications access the multi-billion dollar neuropathic pain market. Extensive consultations with the FDA and DEA on SATIVEX® as a cannabis extract have yielded favorable responses that minimize regulatory concerns. GW Pharmaceuticals (GWP) is seeking an exclusive partner with a strategic focus on pain management to develop and commercialize SATIVEX® in the United States.

BACKGROUND INFORMATION

Pain Market Opportunities

- Patients whose severe cancer pain does not respond to optimized opiate therapy are SATIVEX's initial target market. These, no option patients, represent a U.S. market opportunity of $250 million to $500 million.
- Expected subsequent approvals for diabetic neuropathy, post-herpetic neuropathy and neuropathic pain in multiple sclerosis, represent a multi-billion opportunity.
- Cinical efficacy in opiate-refractory cancer pain patients was demonstrated in a 177 patient European Phase III clinical trial.

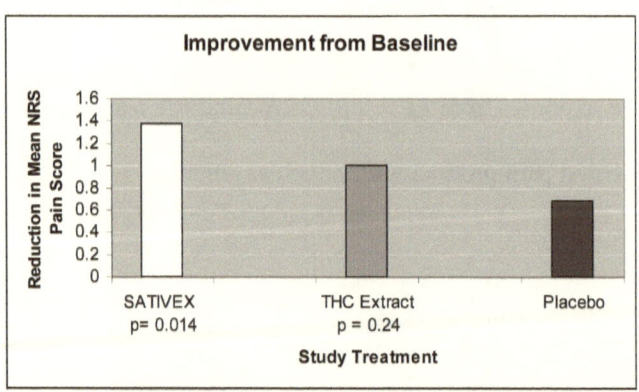

Product

- SATIVEX®, a cannabis-derived oral mucosal spray, is produced using GWP's proprietary technology to grow genetically pure cannabis plants and to extract the active ingredients. GWP manufactures SATIVEX® in tightly controlled, government approved facilities in the UK.
- The oral mucosal spray delivery system allows patients to self-titrate their overall dose and pattern of dosing to meet their individual pain-relief needs.

Clinical/Regulatory

- The FDA's Division of Anesthesia, Analgesia and Rheumatology Products accepted GWP's IND for advanced cancer pain in January, 2006. European Phase III study results were instrumental in the FDA's decision. (Details are in the January 4, 2006 press release, at Appendix A.)
- Protocol for the first Phase III study calls for 250 patients and 5 weeks duration of treatment. The Chief Investigator is Dr. Russell K. Portenoy, Chairman of the Department of Pain Medicine and Palliative Care, Beth Israel Medical Center, New York, New York, one of the world's most important opinion leaders in the treatment of pain.
- The following major parts of the SATIVEX® have been completed: genotoxicology package, repeat dose toxicology, local irritation (single and repeat dose), reproductive toxicology package, safety pharmacology, CYP450 inhibition studies, and carcinogencity studies.
- GWP expects to submit an NDA by mid-2008.
- The FDA and DEA have informed GWP that SATIVEX® will not be considered as medical marijuana. Other plant-derived drugs for pain, e.g., morphine and codeine, are FDA approved and are in wide-spread use.
- SATIVEX®'s formulation and delivery system make abuse of the drug or extraction of its active ingredient virtually impossible.

CRITICAL CONCEPTS—SATIVEX® AS A CANNABINOID PHARMACEUTICAL

- SATIVEX® is a pharmaceutical product that is extracted from cannabis using state-of-the-art industry technology. It is not, and is not treated by the FDA and DEA as, "medical marijuana".

- Cannabinoid drugs are an accepted class of pharmaceuticals. Marinol (active ingredient Δ^9-tetrahydrocannabinol, or THC) has been on the market in the US since 1985 and enjoys DEA Schedule III status.
- SATIVEX® has less abuse potential that Marinol. The cannabidiol component of SATIVEX®, reduces the euphoric and other psychoactive effects of THC. The pharmacokinetic profile of SATIVEX® is one of slow onset and low peak serum levels, exactly the inverse of the profile that produces a euphoric effect.
- With more than five hundred patient-years of exposure in human clinical trials, GWP has seen no evidence of tolerance or abuse and no evidence of diversion. GWP is in the final stages of consulting with the FDA to agree on the design of trials to demonstrate the low potential for abuse.
- GWP maintains excellent relationships with the FDA, DEA and CSS (Controlled Substances Staff), who understand the sound medical and scientific basis for the product, and who have been consulted extensively on all aspects of the development program.
- As evidenced by a recent statement by John Walters, Director of National Drug Control Policy, as well as by the DEA's support for research into medicinal use of cannabis-derived substances, the Federal government recognizes the clear difference between marijuana on the one hand and cannabis-derived, FDA-approved pharmaceuticals on the other. It would be most unlikely for either agency to reverse their publicly stated positions upon SATIVEX receiving FDA approval to commercialize.

INVESTMENT CONSIDERATIONS

Addresses large and underserved markets

Cancer pain affects up to 90% of advanced cancer patients, and up to 42% receive inadequate pain relief from existing medications. The significant medical need for better pain relief options helps assure a receptive marketplace for the first indication for SATIVEX®.

Neuropathic pain is a major and growing market, with an estimated $2.5 billion of global sales in 2004 that is projected to grow to $5.5 billion in 2010. Millions of US patients—prevalence estimates range to 1–2%—suffer neuropathic pain, and existing drugs provide only partial relief.

Low risk clinical trials

Efficacy has been demonstrated in the lead indication and others in European trials. U.S. Phase III clinical trials are expected to produce the same results.

SATIVEX® is approved and marketed in Canada for neuropathic pain in multiple sclerosis.

FDA's Division Director has encouraged GWP to study additional pain indications.

Short time to market

SATIVEX® timeline schedule projects NDA submission for its initial indication in mid-2008.

Limited Competition

GWP's patents along with its proprietary production and manufacturing technology can be expected to provide commercial protection for the foreseeable future.

We know of no competitive new chemical entities in late-stage clinical trials.

Verification of Value

SATIVEX® has been licensed to Almirall in Europe (ex UK) and to Bayer in the UK and Canada. Almirall agreed to a £12 million paid upfront payment and additional milestone payments of up to £34 million. (Details are in the December 12, 2005 press release, at Appendix B.)

APPENDIX A

GW Pharmaceuticals plc, press release 4th January, 2006

FDA Accepts Investigational New Drug (IND) Application For Sativex®

Sativex® To Enter Directly Into Phase III Cancer Pain Trials in United States

GW Pharmaceuticals (AiM:GWP) today announced that the U.S. Food and Drug Administration (FDA) has accepted its Investigational New Drug (IND) Application for Sativex®, a cannabis-derived, oro-mucosal spray composed primarily of tetrahydrocannabinol (THC) and cannabidiol (CBD), a non-psychoactive cannabinoid, for the treatment of pain in patients with advanced cancer that has not been adequately relieved by opioid medications.

As part of this IND, the FDA has agreed that GW Pharmaceuticals may proceed directly into pivotal Phase III clinical trials in the United States in this very seriously ill patient population.

This IND follows a pre-IND/end of Phase II meeting held with the FDA in June 2005. The FDA has reviewed the extensive quality, safety and efficacy data generated by GW on Sativex in Europe. In addition, the FDA has provided written guidance on the U.S. Phase III trial protocol. The planned 250 patient, double-blind, randomized placebo controlled study will evaluate the effect of Sativex in relieving average daily pain, reducing the use of breakthrough opioid medications, improving the quality of sleep and relevant aspects of quality of life among other outcome measures.

Pain is one of the common symptoms associated with cancer and each year more than 250,000 terminal cancer patients in the USA take opioids for pain relief. Approximately 75% of advanced cancer patients experience pain.

"A previous Phase III clinical study showed that Sativex achieved a statistically significant improvement in pain relief in terminally ill cancer patients," says researcher, Dr. Russell K. Portenoy, Chairman of the Department of Pain Medicine and Palliative Care at Beth Israel Medical Center in New York City. "Although opioids are highly effective analgesics, studies suggest that as many as one-third of patients with pain due to advanced cancer do not obtain adequate relief and new treatments are needed. Cannabinoid formulations may represent an important option in the future and the information obtained from clinical trials of Sativex will be critical in defining their role."

APPENDIX B

GW Pharmaceuticals plc, press release 12th December, 2005

GW and Almirall Announce European Development and Marketing Agreement for Sativex®

GW and Almirall Prodesfarma, S.A. ("Almirall") announce that they have entered into an exclusive agreement for Almirall to market Sativex® in Europe (excluding the UK).

Sativex is being developed by GW and is a novel prescription pharmaceutical product derived from components of the cannabis plant. Sativex is administered via a spray into the mouth. In April 2005, Canada became the first country in the world to approve Sativex as a prescription medicine.

Under the terms of the agreement, GW has maintained a significant share of long term product revenues whilst benefiting from a £12 million signature fee. In addition, milestone payments are payable on the successful completion of each of the ongoing pivotal Phase III trials, as well as on regulatory approvals and in relation to achievement of sales targets. Including the signature fee, milestones payable under the contract may total up to £46 million.

Almirall is Spain's largest pharmaceutical company and one of Europe's leading private pharmaceutical companies, with 2005 sales approaching 1 billion euros. Almirall is headquartered in Barcelona, and has a staff of over 3,200 people, approximately 500 of whom form part of the R&D team. It is currently present in around 100 countries worldwide and has a portfolio of proprietary and licensed products. The company has a significant presence in Spain, where it is number two by market share, and subsidiary operations in other major European markets, including France, Germany, Italy, Portugal and Belgium. Almirall is currently strengthening its direct presence in Europe and Latin America via affiliates, and is actively looking for in-licensing opportunities to support this strategy, medicines for the Central Nervous System being one of its priority areas.

Sativex is in Phase III trials for the treatment of Multiple Sclerosis symptoms (neuropathic pain and spasticity), neuropathic pain (peripheral and general) and cancer pain. Under the agreement GW is responsible for completing the development of Sativex for these three indications.

In addition to the three initial target indications, Almirall and GW expect to collaborate on the development of Sativex in other indications. The parties will be discussing potential new indications over the coming months. It is anticipated that Almirall will contribute to the cost of development of new indications.

The licensed territory includes the members of the European Union (excluding the UK), EU accession countries as well as Switzerland, Norway and Turkey. In countries where Almirall has no direct presence at the time of product launch, the companies shall jointly agree the appointment of distribution partners. In such countries, GW may elect to distribute the product itself. In the UK, Sativex is already licensed to Bayer HealthCare.

GW shall be the Marketing Authorisation holder for Sativex. In addition, GW is to be responsible for commercial product supply and will manage the supply of product through a range of contract manufacturing partners, arrangements for which are all in place and being utilised to supply commercial product to Canada.

Following receipt of the signature fee, GW's financial position has been significantly strengthened, with net cash balances now totalling £22 million.

Dr Geoffrey Guy, Executive Chairman of GW, said: "We are delighted to have entered into this agreement with Almirall. As one of the leading specialist European pharmaceutical companies, Almirall is exactly the profile of partner that we have been seeking for Sativex. We look forward to working together in building a successful long term collaboration and to realising the market potential for Sativex across all its potential indications. GW's commercial strategy is to maximise the value of Sativex by retaining a significant interest in revenues from product sales whilst at the same time generating sizeable cash payments in the short term to meet GW's financial requirements. The terms of this agreement reflect the merits of this strategy."

Dr Jorge Gallardo, President-CEO of Almirall, said: "We are very pleased with this agreement for Sativex with GW Pharmaceuticals. GW has proven to be an innovative company with a strong scientific basis. This partnership represents a step forward for Almirall reinforcing our presence in European markets, and is a key milestone in our aim of offering society innovative medicines to fulfill unmet medical needs. Our challenge is to improve the health and quality of life of patients suffering from MS and other debilitating conditions."

INDEX